CW00400591

The Moonstone

LEVEL THREE   1000 HEADWORDS

OXFORD
UNIVERSITY PRESS

Great Clarendon Street, Oxford OX2 6DP

Oxford University Press is a department of the University of Oxford.
It furthers the University's objective of excellence in research, scholarship,
and education by publishing worldwide in

Oxford New York

Auckland Cape Town Dar es Salaam Hong Kong Karachi
Kuala Lumpur Madrid Melbourne Mexico City Nairobi
New Delhi Shanghai Taipei Toronto

With offices in

Argentina Austria Brazil Chile Czech Republic France Greece
Guatemala Hungary Italy Japan Poland Portugal Singapore
South Korea Switzerland Thailand Turkey Ukraine Vietnam

OXFORD and OXFORD ENGLISH are registered trade marks of
Oxford University Press in the UK and in certain other countries

This edition © Oxford University Press 2010

The moral rights of the author have been asserted

Database right Oxford University Press (maker)

First published in Dominoes 2006

2014 2013 2012 2011 2010

10 9 8 7 6 5 4 3

ISBN: 978 0 19 424821 1 BOOK
ISBN: 978 0 19 424779 5 BOOK AND MULTIROM PACK
MULTIROM NOT AVAILABLE SEPARATELY

No unauthorized photocopying

Printed in China

This book is printed on paper from certified and well-managed sources.

ACKNOWLEDGEMENTS

Illustrations by: Sally Wern Comport

The publisher would like to thank the following for permission to reproduce photographs: Alamy
Images pp6 (Ganesh Hindu elephant God Golden sculpture/J Marshall/Tribaleye Images),
46 (Hindu statue/World Religions Photo Library), 72 (Drum/Yadid Levy), 72 (Fire/Maximilian
Weinzierl); Bridgeman Art Library Ltd p74 (The Hope Diamond/Smithsonian Institution,
Washington DC, USA); Corbis pp71 (Sir Arthur Conan Doyle/Bettmann), 72 (Fireworks/Alan
Schein), 72 (Row of elephants/Lindsay Hebberd), 72 (Bonfire ash/Charles O'Rear), 73 (Face
painting/Manjunath Kiran/epa); Cultural Heritage Online p76 (The Regent Pitt diamond/
Droits reserves); Getty Images pp72 (Powder paint/Phil Degginger), 74 (Evalyn Walsh/
Topical Press Agency/Stringer); Natural History Museum Picture Library pp15 (Yellow
gemstone), 76 (Kor-i-noor/Frank Greenaway); OUP p27 (Beach/Carl & Ann Purcell); RIA
Novosti Photolibrary p75 (Orlof diamond); TopFoto p71 (Agatha Christie); TROPIX Photo
Library pp72 (Decorated elephant/Dominic Jenkin), 72 (Row of elephants/Dominic Jenkin).

Cover: Courtesy of BBC Information & Archives

DOMINOES

Series Editors: Bill Bowler and Sue Parminter

The Moonstone

Wilkie Collins

Text adaptation by Merinda Wilson

Illustrated by Sally Wern Comport

Wilkie Collins (1824–1889) was born in London, the son of a successful painter. He started writing in his twenties, and his first novel was published in 1850. Ten years later he published his first really successful book, *The Woman in White* (available in The Oxford Bookworms Library), a mystery thriller. *The Moonstone* (1868) is often described as the first detective novel, and has been filmed several times.

OXFORD
UNIVERSITY PRESS

BEFORE READING

1 **Read about the characters from *The Moonstone* below. Complete the sentences with these words: *cousin, cousin, mother, parents, uncle, uncle* and *aunt*.**

> Rachel is the daughter of Lady Julia Verinder. Her father died when she was a child.
>
> John Herncastle is Lady Verinder's brother. He fought for Britain in India.
>
> Lady Verinder has two sisters. Her sister, Adelaide, married rich Mr Blake and they had a son, Franklin. Adelaide died when Franklin was a child.
>
> Lady Verinder's second sister, Caroline, married Mr Ablewhite, a banker. They have a son, Godfrey, and live in the town near Lady Verinder.

a Lady Verinder is Rachel's ....

b John Herncastle is Rachel's ....

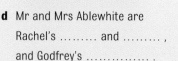

c Franklin is Rachel's ....

d Mr and Mrs Ablewhite are Rachel's .... and ...., and Godfrey's ....

e Godfrey is Rachel's ....

2 **The Moonstone is a mystery story about a diamond that brings bad luck. What do you think happens to the characters above in the story?**

a Who steals the Moonstone diamond? . . . .

b Who does Rachel marry? . . . .

c Who dies in the story? . . . .

Prologue

Seringapatam, India (1799)

I am writing to you, the family, from India to explain why I am no longer friendly with my cousin, John Herncastle.

Herncastle and I were here with the British **army**. We were staying near the Palace of Seringapatam in southern India. There were many mysterious stories about the palace. One of the wildest stories was about a yellow **diamond**. It was once part of a **statue** of the Moon God, and it was **guarded** day and night by three Indian **priests**. But a hundred years ago the diamond – called the Moonstone – was stolen and brought to the Palace of Seringapatam. People said that three priests were secretly still guarding the Moonstone at the palace. Herncastle was one of the few men in the army who thought that the Moonstone story was true.

On the 4th of May 1799, the British army **attacked** the palace. On the night of the attack, I found Herncastle in one of the palace rooms with a bloody knife in his hand. Lying across the entrance of the room there were the dead bodies of two Indians, and in front of him another Indian was falling to the floor. As the Indian lay dying, he looked at Herncastle and said:

'The Moonstone will have its **revenge** on you and yours!'

At that moment, the room filled with more men, the fighting went on, and I didn't see my cousin until the next morning.

'Tell me,' I said, 'how did the Indian die and what did his last words mean?'

'I know no more than you do,' said Herncastle.

I turned my back on him and we have not spoken since.

Please understand that I'm writing about my cousin in order to warn you. I did not see him kill the men with my own eyes, but I am quite sure that he did kill them. Not only this, but I am also sure that he stole the Moonstone. The Moonstone will have its revenge on Herncastle and any other person to whom he gives the diamond.

---

army a large number of people who fight for their country

diamond a very bright, hard stone that looks like glass and is very expensive

statue a picture of a person made of metal or stone

guard to look after a place and stop people attacking it

priest a man who works in a temple

attack to start fighting

revenge something that you do to hurt someone because they have hurt you

Chapter 1
An Indian diamond in Yorkshire

On the twenty-fourth of May, 1848, Lady Verinder called her old **servant** Gabriel Betteredge into the sitting room of her family home in Yorkshire.

'Gabriel,' she said. 'Here is news that will surprise you. Franklin Blake has come back from **abroad**. He is coming tomorrow to stay until next month, and will be here for Rachel's birthday. You must get a room ready for him.'

Franklin Blake was Lady Verinder's **nephew**, her eldest sister's only son. He had lived with his aunt and his cousin Rachel Verinder in Yorkshire as a boy, until he went to school in Germany. This was Franklin's first visit back, and everyone was excited about seeing him again.

The next morning, Lady Verinder and Miss Rachel drove out to lunch with some friends because Franklin had told them he wasn't arriving until dinner time. Betteredge was getting the room ready for Franklin when he heard a noise in the garden. He went outside and saw three dark-skinned Indians looking at the house. With them was a small, fair English boy. They wanted to see the lady of the house but left politely when they were told that she was out.

Shortly afterwards, Betteredge's daughter, Penelope, came in a hurry to see her father. She also worked at Lady Verinder's house as Rachel's servant.

'Father,' she cried, 'Where are those Indians? They want to do something **wicked**, I'm sure.'

Penelope had followed the Indians when they entered the garden. One Indian made the small boy hold out his hand. He put some black **ink** on it, and asked:

'Will the English gentleman travel to this house this evening? Has the English gentleman got *it* with him?'

The boy's answer to both questions had been 'Yes'.

servant a person who works for someone rich

abroad in or to another country

nephew your sister's (or brother's) son

wicked very bad

ink you put this in a pen in order to write with it

Betteredge promised his daughter to ask Franklin Blake what the 'it' in the conversation was. Then he went to fetch the **housemaid**, Rosanna Spearman, for lunch. Rosanna was quiet and hardworking, and Betteredge liked her. He also knew her secret. Rosanna had been a thief, and she had been to prison. But Lady Verinder had felt sorry for her and had given her a job as a housemaid, so Rosanna didn't need to steal in order to get money any more.

Betteredge followed Rosanna's favourite walk to a lonely beach not far from the house. The place was known as the **Shivering Sand** because the moving sands there were dangerous when the sea was low. When Betteredge reached the beach, he saw Rosanna in her big grey coat. She was crying.

'Come and sit down,' he said kindly, 'and tell me why you always come to this miserable place.'

'I try to keep away, but I can't,' she said in a low voice.

Suddenly there was a shout from behind them. 'Betteredge! Where are you?'

Rosanna looked around. 'Oh! Who is it?' she asked softly.

A bright-eyed young gentleman came up to them. He was not a tall man, but he was very good-looking. He had brown hair and a

housemaid a woman who cleans and works in a rich person's house

shiver to move quickly from side to side, often because something makes you feel afraid or cold

sand it is yellow, and we find a lot of it on the beach

'Betteredge! Where are you?'

3

beard, and he wore fashionable, foreign clothes. He came and sat down on the sand next to the old man. It was Franklin Blake, and he was four hours early!

'Welcome back, Mr Franklin,' the old servant said.

Betteredge was pleasantly surprised to see the man whom he had last seen as a boy. But Rosanna Spearman's face turned deep red. She seemed suddenly uncomfortable and she ran back to the house.

'You have arrived early,' continued Betteredge.

'I have a reason for that,' the young man answered. 'I wanted to lose a dark stranger who has been following me.'

Betteredge, told Franklin about the visit by the three Indians. He was surprised by Franklin's reply.

'"Has the English gentleman got *it* with him?" I suppose that "it" means *this*,' he said, and he pulled something out of his pocket. 'My uncle's famous Indian diamond.'

'Oh, sir! Why do you have your wicked uncle's diamond with you?' asked Betteredge.

'My uncle has left his diamond as a birthday present to his **niece**, my cousin Rachel,' said Franklin. 'And my father asked me to bring it here. But, Betteredge, why do you call my uncle wicked? What do you know about him?'

'Lady Verinder's brother, John Herncastle, was in India with the army, and returned to England with a large diamond. From the moment of his return, all his family refused to see him, and no one ever knew the true story of how he had got his diamond.'

'Your uncle never tried to sell the **jewel** and he never showed it to anyone. Twice in India he nearly died, and he thought that the Moonstone held a terrible secret.'

Betteredge told Franklin all this as they sat near the Shivering Sand. He also spoke of a visit from Herncastle two years before, on Rachel's birthday. At that time Lady Verinder had refused to let her brother into the house. 'I shall remember my niece's birthday!' Herncastle laughed wickedly and he left.

niece your sister's (or brother's) daughter

jewel an expensive stone

Franklin listened with greater and greater interest to Betteredge's story.

'Now let me tell you what I know,' Franklin said. 'My father's business with the Herncastle diamond is a strange story. My uncle gave my father some important papers, and in return, my father put the jewel in his bank and told his **lawyer**, Mr Bruff, that he would get a note from Herncastle once a year. If Bruff didn't get a note on an agreed date, it was because someone had murdered Herncastle. Bruff then had orders to read a letter which was left with the diamond.'

'After my uncle died in his sleep six months ago, Bruff opened the letter. It told him to take the Moonstone secretly to Amsterdam and have it cut into four to six stones. I think my uncle's life had been in danger from people who were looking for the Moonstone. And he thought he could stop the danger if the diamond were no longer a single stone.'

'But then, in his **will**, my uncle left the Moonstone as a birthday present to his niece, but only if her mother, Lady Verinder, was still alive. Why? For me the important question is: Does the terrible secret of the Moonstone continue after Herncastle dies?'

'Did Herncastle say why he left the diamond to Miss Rachel?' Betteredge asked.

'Oh, yes,' replied Franklin, 'His will says that it is to show that he **forgives** Lady Verinder. But remember that Lady Verinder refused to see her brother for years!'

'I don't know what to do for the best,' said Franklin. 'What do you think, Betteredge?'

Betteredge's idea was to put the diamond into a bank at Frizinghall, the nearest town. It was a month until Miss Rachel's birthday, and in this way they could wait and see what happened.

'A wonderful idea,' Franklin said and he jumped up. 'Get the best horse ready for me. I shall take the diamond to Frizinghall before the ladies come back.'

lawyer someone who works to help people with the law

will the paper that you write and sign, which says how you want to divide your money between people in your family when you die

forgive (*past* **forgave, forgiven**) to stop being angry with someone for something bad that they did

5

READING CHECK

Tick the boxes to complete the sentences.

a The story begins in . . .
1 ☐ Germany.
2 ☑ India.
3 ☐ Yorkshire.

b The Moonstone is a valuable jewel that belonged to . . .
1 ☐ Franklin Blake.
2 ☐ John Herncastle.
3 ☐ an Indian priest.

c Franklin Blake is Lady Verinder's . . .
1 ☐ nephew.
2 ☐ son.
3 ☐ uncle.

d Before Rosanna Spearman came to work at Lady Verinder's house she . . .
1 ☐ worked in a bank.
2 ☐ lived in India.
3 ☐ was in prison.

e Lady Verinder refused to speak to her brother, John Herncastle, because . . .
1 ☐ he had attacked the Palace of Seringapatam.
2 ☐ he had done wicked things in India.
3 ☐ his life had been in danger.

f Franklin Blake was told to give the Moonstone to Rachel as a birthday present from . . .
1 ☐ John Herncastle.
2 ☐ Franklin's father.
3 ☐ Mr Bruff.

g Franklin and Betteredge decide to take the Moonstone . . .
1 ☐ back to London.
2 ☐ to the Shivering Sand.
3 ☐ to the bank in Frizinghall.

WORD WORK

1 Use the words round the statue to complete the sentences on page 7.

shiver

army

sand

will

revenge

forgive

abroad

attacked

ink

a I was alone at home, and the noise of the wind made me ... _shiver_ ... .

b My brother's going to join the .... and fight for his country.

c We prefer to go .... for our holidays.

d This is an old pen; you need to fill it with .... before you can write with it.

e The .... on the beach wasn't yellow, it was white.

f Tom died without a ...., so they didn't know how to divide his money.

g Herncastle wanted .... on his family for the bad things they had done to him.

h Last week in our street someone was .... and his money was stolen.

i If you say sorry for losing my diamond ring, then I'll .... you.

2 Use words from Chapter 1 to complete the definitions.

a A _lawyer_ works with the law and tells people what they can and cannot do.

b A _ _ _ _ _ _ is someone who works in a temple or a church.

c A _ _ _ _ _ _ _ _ _ is a young woman who looks after a rich person's house.

d A _ _ _ _ _ looks after a building and stops other people stealing things from it.

e A _ _ _ _ _ _ _ is a man or woman who works for a rich person.

f A _ _ _ _ _ _ is the son of your sister or brother.

g A _ _ _ _ _ is the daughter of your sister or brother.

GUESS WHAT

What do you think happens in the next chapter? Match the names with the sentences.

Betteredge Franklin Lady Verinder Rachel Rosanna

a .... falls in love with Franklin.

b .... wears the Moonstone on her dress.

c .... is angry about John Herncastle's birthday gift to Rachel.

d .... stops smoking to please Rachel.

e .... and .... want to send Rosanna away.

Chapter 2

The diamond disappears

Betteredge and Franklin hurried back to the house, and found a good horse to take Franklin to Frizinghall. He rode away at once to take the Moonstone to the bank there.

When Lady Verinder and Miss Rachel came back later that afternoon, they were surprised to hear that their **guest** had arrived early and then left for Frizinghall. Being careful not to say anything about the diamond, Betteredge explained that Franklin had suddenly changed his plans.

Just then, Betteredge's daughter, Penelope, came to talk to him. 'Father,' she said. 'Since Rosanna Spearman returned from the Shivering Sand, she has been **behaving** very strangely. Has she ever met Mr Blake before?'

'No, never,' replied Betteredge.

'Then I think,' said Penelope, 'that Rosanna has fallen in love with Franklin Blake!'

Betteredge laughed loudly. How could a poor housemaid like Rosanna fall in love with a gentleman like Franklin?

But Penelope wasn't laughing. 'Father! You're wicked to make fun of Rosanna,' she said angrily, and left the room.

When the diamond was safely in the bank, Franklin returned from Frizinghall. The ladies were pleased to have him with them that evening. Rachel took special care to get ready for dinner, and after dinner she sang with Franklin while Lady Verinder played the piano. At the end of the evening, Betteredge brought Franklin some **brandy** and water to his room. He could see that Franklin was no longer worried about the diamond.

'Miss Rachel is the most **charming** girl that I have seen since I came back to England!' said Franklin dreamily.

There was still nearly a month until Rachel's birthday party. To pass the time, Franklin gave Rachel the idea of **painting** the door into her **sitting room**, the room next to her bedroom. Franklin

guest a person that you invite to your home

behave to do or say things in a certain way

brandy a strong alcoholic drink

charming nice to other people

paint to put different colours on something

sitting room a room in a house where people sit and talk

and Rachel started painting flowers, birds, and small animals around the door. While the two of them were busy painting every day, the servants were busy talking about them. Everyone could see that Franklin was in love with Rachel. He had even stopped smoking to please her. But what did Rachel feel for him?

Rachel was indeed a charming young woman. She was small and very pretty, with black hair, dark eyes, and the most beautiful

The two of them were busy painting every day.

smile. But Rachel was different from most of the young women of her age, because she was strong and **determined**. She was able to decide things for herself, and did not need to ask other people what to do. She was also very honest, and had never told a lie in her life. But it was impossible to find out who Rachel loved; Rachel did not tell her secrets to anyone, not even her mother.

Another guest who was coming to the party was Rachel's cousin, Godfrey Ablewhite. He was a tall, fine-looking man with long, fair hair. He worked in London as a lawyer, but was also well-known for his **charity** work which helped poor women. He was a good speaker at meetings and people were happy to give him lots of money for charity. In fact, Godfrey was popular with everyone. Rachel had a photograph of him beside her bed.

A few days before the party, the housemaid Rosanna Spearman was behaving very strangely and looked ill. Lady Verinder told Betteredge to send her away for a rest. But Rosanna cried and cried, and refused to leave. Finally, Lady Verinder agreed with Betteredge that it was better to let Rosanna stay on at the house.

It was the 21st of June; the day of Rachel's eighteenth birthday. After he had painted the door all morning with Rachel, Franklin rode off to Frizinghall to fetch the Moonstone. He returned with Godfrey Ablewhite and his two sisters, who had also been invited to the party. They were talking excitedly as they entered the house.

'Have you got the diamond safe?' Betteredge asked Franklin quietly.

'Yes, it's here in my pocket,' replied Franklin.

'Did you see any Indians?' continued Betteredge.

'No,' said Franklin calmly, and he walked across the hall to look for Rachel.

Half an hour later, there were loud cries of excitement from the library. In the middle of the room sat Rachel with **Colonel** Herncastle's diamond in her hand. Franklin had just given it to

determined
having decided to do something

charity helping poor people

colonel an important soldier in the army

her, and Godfrey and his sisters were staring at it.

'How wonderful!' the sisters cried.

'Beautiful! Beautiful!' said Godfrey softly.

The diamond was the size of a small bird's egg. A beautiful yellow light shone from the centre of the jewel like bright sunlight.

Lady Verinder was standing by the window, with her back to the others. Why had her brother left this gift for Rachel? Had he forgiven Lady Verinder, or was he looking for revenge?

That afternoon Rachel and Godfrey took a walk in the garden. They had not seen each other for some time, and they walked arm-in-arm, laughing. But when they returned to the house half an hour later, they walked separately, and they were not laughing. Godfrey had asked Rachel to marry him, but Rachel had refused; she had explained to him that she was in love with another man.

Later that evening, Rachel wore the diamond at the dinner party. As the guests came in, they looked at Rachel and her diamond with great excitement and interest. The fact that Rachel had chosen to wear the diamond at the party only made Lady Verinder more worried.

When all the guests had arrived, they took their places at the dinner table. The guest on Rachel's left was Dr Candy, the doctor at Frizinghall.

'I would like to do an **experiment** on your diamond, Rachel,' said Dr Candy. 'If I burn your diamond, it may disappear, and you won't need to worry about keeping it safe!' he laughed.

But the guest who was sitting on Rachel's right was much more serious. Mr Murthwaite was a tall, thin, quiet man. He had travelled all over India for many years, and he knew everything about the country and its people. He did not speak much during the party, but when he did speak, it was to say something about the diamond.

'Be very careful, Miss Rachel,' he said. 'If you ever go to India, don't wear that diamond. In a certain Indian city, if the priests see

experiment
something that you try to see what will happen

you with the Moonstone, they will kill you.'

'Oh, how interesting!' cried Rachel and the Ablewhite sisters.

But the conversation at the table did not go well. Dr Candy and Franklin started arguing about medicine. Although Franklin had been sleeping badly, he refused to take any medicine. He told Dr Candy that all medicines, and the doctors who gave them, were useless! Franklin spoke loudly in front of the other guests and his words made Dr Candy angry.

Their argument only stopped in the end because there were noises in the garden.

At once all the guests went outside, where they saw three Indians and a small English boy dancing on the grass. Betteredge recognized them immediately as the Indians he had seen the day that Franklin had arrived. The ladies were amused by the strange music and the dancing of the Indians, until Murthwaite spoke to them in their own language. No one understood what he said, but the Indians quickly left the garden and the guests went back into the house.

Murthwaite stopped to talk to Franklin and Betteredge.

'Those Indians are not dancers. I am sure that they are priests,' warned Murthwaite. 'They saw the Moonstone on Miss Rachel's dress and they will do anything to get it back. Your lives are in great danger!'

'What shall we do?' asked Franklin.

'You must take the diamond to Amsterdam and have it cut into smaller stones. The danger of the Moonstone will end when it is cut up,' replied Murthwaite.

'I will talk to Lady Verinder about it first thing in the morning,' said Franklin.

❖

When all the other guests had gone home, Lady Verinder, Rachel, and the two gentlemen were sitting in the library. Godfrey was drinking brandy and water, but Franklin didn't have anything. He looked tired, and he was worried about the diamond. Lady Verinder was worried, too.

'Rachel, where are you going to put the diamond tonight?' she asked.

'In the Indian **cabinet** in my sitting-room,' Rachel replied.

'But there's no lock on the cabinet,' said Lady Verinder.

'Why are you worried about that?' asked Rachel. 'Are there thieves in the house?'

Lady Verinder saw that her daughter was determined, so she said goodnight to everyone and went up to bed. Then Rachel, too, stood up to go. She shook hands politely with Godfrey, but smiled at Franklin before she left the room.

After that the gentlemen went to bed. Franklin was still worried about the diamond, and he asked Betteredge to send some brandy and water to his room to help him sleep. After that, Betteredge made sure that all the doors and windows were safely locked, and finally, he too went to bed.

At eight o'clock the next morning, Penelope took Rachel's morning tea to her room as usual. When she entered the sitting-room, Rachel was already up. She was staring at the Indian cabinet – the diamond was not there.

Penelope ran to Betteredge's room. 'Father, Father!' she cried, 'The diamond has gone!'

Betteredge hurried to Rachel's sitting-room. Rachel was standing next to the empty cabinet, her face white.

'The diamond has gone,' said Rachel quietly. 'Please go away, now. I want to be alone.'

Rachel went into her bedroom, locked the door and refused to talk to anyone. Rachel's **behaviour** surprised everyone in the house. She had never been very interested in expensive jewels, but now she seemed to be deeply **troubled** by the loss of the Moonstone. Lady Verinder was also troubled; a jewel worth over £20,000 had disappeared from her house. Was this her brother's revenge?

cabinet a small cupboard where you keep interesting things for people to see

behaviour the way that you do and say things

troubled worried

READING CHECK

1 What happened on the day of Rachel's birthday? Put these sentences in the correct order and number them 1–9.

a ☐ Franklin gives the Moonstone to Rachel.

b ☐ Dr Candy and Franklin argue at dinner.

c ☐ Godfrey asks Rachel to marry him, but she refuses.

d ☐ Franklin and Rachel work together on the door of Rachel's sitting room.

e ☐ Murthwaite warns Franklin and Betteredge that the Moonstone may bring danger.

f ☐ Godfrey Ablewhite and his sisters arrive at the house.

g ☐ The guests go into the garden to watch the Indian dancers.

h ☐ Rachel wears the Moonstone on her dress at the party.

i ☐ Franklin rides to Frizinghall to fetch the diamond.

2 Are these sentences true or false? Tick the boxes.

		True	False
a	Penelope thinks that Franklin Blake has fallen in love with Rosanna Spearman.	☐	☑
b	Franklin gives up smoking because he wants to please Rachel.	☐	☐
c	People give money to Godfrey Ablewhite for his charity work because he is good-looking.	☐	☐
d	Lady Verinder is unhappy about her brother's birthday gift for Rachel.	☐	☐
e	At the dinner party, Franklin is angry with Dr Candy because he wants to do an experiment with Rachel's diamond.	☐	☐
f	The Indian dancers leave the garden when Betteredge speaks to them.	☐	☐
g	Rachel isn't worried that the Indian cabinet doesn't have a lock.	☐	☐

WORD WORK

Find the words round the diamond to complete Betteredge's diary.

behaviourcharminggguestscharitytroubledpaintingColonedetermiinedbehavingsitting room

19th June, 1848 — Diary

It's nearly Rachel's birthday and I have to prepare the rooms for the **(a)** guests. Godfrey Ablewhite and his sisters are coming. Godfrey is a fine speaker and lots of people give him money for **(b)** .... Rachel and Franklin have been **(c)** .... the door of her **(d)** .... They make a **(e)** .... couple, but they are very different. Rachel is **(f)** .... but Franklin never knows what to do. I don't know what to do about Rosanna. She has been **(g)** .... very strangely. Lady Verinder is very **(h)** ...., too, by her strange **(i)** .... I wonder what she will think when she sees **(j)** .... Herncastle's gift to Rachel.

GUESS WHAT

What do you think happens in the next chapter? Tick three boxes.

a ☐ Franklin goes to Frizinghall to fetch the police.

b ☐ They search Rosanna Spearman's room and find the diamond.

c ☐ They search Rachel's sitting room but they can't find the diamond.

d ☐ Rachel helps the police to find her diamond.

e ☐ Franklin writes to his father to ask him to send a detective from London.

f ☐ The Indian dancers find the diamond and take it back to India.

Chapter 3

The investigation

Franklin Blake immediately **suspected** that the Indians who had been at the house the day before had taken the stone. Betteredge agreed that they were interested in the Moonstone, but he had locked all the doors and windows before he went to bed. It had not been possible for anyone to get into – or out of – the house that night.

Franklin went to Frizinghall to speak to the police, and later that morning Detective Seagrave arrived at the house. Seagrave suspected that one of the servants had taken the jewel, and he put his policemen to guard their rooms. Then he went to Rachel's sitting room to begin the **investigation**. All the servants hurried after him to **protest** about the policemen in front of their room doors. But Seagrave told them to leave him alone.

'And be more careful!' he said as he pointed to a **smear** in the paint work at the bottom of the sitting room door. 'Look what you've done with your skirts!'

The servants left and the detective continued to **examine** Rachel's room. Suddenly Rachel came out of her bedroom and said to Detective Seagrave: 'I don't want you here. My diamond is lost and you will never find it!'

❖

The detective's search did not find one **clue**. Franklin decided to ask his father to send a better policeman from London. He called Betteredge to the library. When Betteredge arrived, Rosanna Spearman was coming out of the library door. Betteredge waited for her to leave and then went into the room.

'Ah, Betteredge,' said Franklin. 'Get a horse ready for me. I need to take this letter to Frizinghall. But,' he continued, 'before you go, I must say that Rosanna seems to know a lot about the Moonstone.'

'Why? What did she say?' asked Betteredge carefully. He did not want to say anything about Rosanna's past life as a thief or her time in prison.

suspect to think that someone has done something wrong

investigation something that a detective does to understand how or why a crime has happened

protest something that you do to say or show that you do not like something; to say or show that you do not like something

smear a mark that is made by moving against paint when it is still wet

examine to look carefully at something

clue something that helps you to understand a mystery or a crime

'She said, "They will never find the diamond, nor the person who took it!" and then she smiled at me! What does she mean?'

'I don't know, sir, but I will talk to Lady Verinder about it.'

Betteredge left to get a horse ready for Franklin. As he went past the dining room, he noticed that Rosanna was not eating lunch with the others. She had told them she was feeling ill and had gone to her room to lie down.

Later that afternoon, Franklin rode over to Frizinghall to send the letter to his father. And that same afternoon, a woman who looked very like Rosanna Spearman was seen walking quickly along the road to Frizinghall.

❖

The next day, Detective **Sergeant** Cuff arrived from London on the morning train.

'Sergeant Cuff – the best detective in the country!' thought Franklin.

Sergeant Cuff was a very serious man. He had grey hair, wore a dark suit and a white tie, and he never smiled. Cuff went immediately to examine Rachel's room. He soon noticed the smear near the bottom of the painted door.

'Interesting,' said Cuff. 'Someone has walked past the door and made this smear, with a long skirt perhaps, or a **nightgown**. I wonder when this happened? When was the door painted and how long does the paint take to dry?'

'We painted this bit of the door on Wednesday, Rachel's birthday,' explained Franklin. 'We finished at three o'clock in the afternoon. The paint takes twelve hours to dry.'

At that moment, Rachel **burst out** of her bedroom. She stared angrily at Franklin, and spoke to Sergeant Cuff: 'Do not allow this man to help you in your investigation!'

'Thank you for your help, Miss Rachel,' said Cuff calmly. 'And do you know anything about this smear on the door?'

'No!' said Rachel, and she went back into her bedroom.

Penelope had been the last person to go into Rachel's room on

sergeant an important policeman

nightgown a long dress that men and women used to wear to go to bed

burst out (*past* **burst out**) to come out of something, or to start to do something, suddenly

the night the Moonstone disappeared. Sergeant Cuff went to ask her about the smear.

'I left Miss Rachel's room at midnight,' said Penelope. 'There was no smear on the door then. And I was very careful with my skirts not to make a smear!'

'I see,' said Cuff. 'So the smear was made between midnight, when Miss Rachel went to bed on the night of her birthday, and three o'clock on Thursday morning. I think we have an important clue here.'

Sergeant Cuff went to speak to Lady Verinder. 'We must find out who, or what, made the smear on Rachel's door,' he said.

'And then will we find the thief?' asked Lady Verinder.

'At the moment, Madam, I do not say that the diamond was stolen. I say only that the diamond is missing. When we find the clothes that have paint on them, we will learn where the diamond is. I need to examine the clothes of everyone who stayed here on the night of the party.'

Lady Verinder agreed, but Rachel refused to let anyone examine her clothes. If Rachel did not agree, then it was useless for Cuff to examine other people's clothes. He stopped his search for the paint smear and decided to speak to all of the servants, one by one. He found out that on Thursday evening, the night after the Moonstone had disappeared, there had been a light on in Rosanna Spearman's room all night. Did her nightgown have paint on it? Was she making a new nightgown to hide the fact?

That afternoon, Cuff saw Rosanna walking away from the house and he decided to follow her. She went into a small **cottage** in a fishing village not far from the Shivering Sand. The cottage was the home of a fisherman called Yolland, and his daughter, Lucy, and Rosanna were close friends. When Rosanna left the cottage she was carrying something under her coat, and she walked quickly towards the Shivering Sand.

cottage a small house in the country

Later that evening, before it got dark, Sergeant Cuff went back to the fisherman's cottage and asked about Rosanna's visit.

'Rosanna came here this afternoon to write a letter,' explained Mrs Yolland. 'She told me that she is going to leave her job with Lady Verinder! I don't know what the poor girl will do. She asked me for some things to help her move. I gave her a small box, like the one that sailors use to keep their maps dry, and a heavy **chain**. She said that she wanted the chain for her luggage.'

He decided to follow her.

Sergeant Cuff thanked Mrs Yolland for her help, and went back to the house. He knew that Rosanna had been a thief, but he did not suspect that she had stolen the diamond. The person that he suspected was Rachel herself; she had lost her diamond, but did nothing to help the investigation to find it. He thought that Rachel had probably asked Rosanna to help her hide the jewel.

That night, Betteredge was walking across the hall to lock the front door, when Franklin ran out of the library.

'Betteredge,' Franklin said in a worried voice. 'There's something wrong with Rosanna. She came into the library just now and she wanted to tell me something. I'm sorry to say this, Betteredge, but I think that perhaps she wanted to tell me that she had stolen the diamond!'

Both Franklin and Betteredge knew that Rachel's behaviour had been **suspicious**. But it was easier for the family to suspect that a poor servant like Rosanna had taken the diamond, than the young lady of the house.

'I wish to God that the Moonstone had never found its way into this house,' replied Betteredge.

chain a long string of metal that is very strong

suspicious when you think something shows that someone has done something bad

READING CHECK

Choose the best answer to complete the sentences.

a The servants are angry with Detective Seagrave because he . . .

1 ☐ doesn't find any clues.

2 ☑ thinks that one of them has stolen the diamond.

3 ☐ notices the paint smear on the door of Rachel's sitting room.

b Rachel . . .

1 ☐ tries to help the investigation.

2 ☐ doesn't want to help the investigation.

3 ☐ tells Sergeant Cuff about the paint smear on her door.

c The paint smear is an important clue because . . .

1 ☐ Cuff needs to examine everyone's clothes.

2 ☐ it was made after midnight.

3 ☐ it can show the person that took the Moonstone.

d Rosanna went to the Yollands' cottage . . .

1 ☐ to hide the Moonstone.

2 ☐ to see her friend Lucy.

3 ☐ to write a letter.

e Sergeant Cuff thinks that . . .

1 ☐ Rachel knows where the Moonstone is.

2 ☐ Rosanna stole the Moonstone.

3 ☐ the Moonstone is at the Yollands' cottage.

f Franklin is worried about Rosanna because . . .

1 ☐ she is ill.

2 ☐ she wants to tell him something.

3 ☐ he is in love with her.

WORD WORK

Find words from Chapter 3 to match the underlined words in these sentences.

a Detective Seagrave is the first to notice the <u>mark made by moving against wet paint</u> on Rachel's door. ...smear....

b Franklin <u>thinks that something wrong was done by</u> the Indians. ....

c Detective Seagrave starts to <u>look carefully in</u> Rachel's room. ....

d Franklin is very happy when Sergeant Cuff comes to continue the <u>finding out of how the crime happened</u>. ....

e Rosanna wants a <u>long string of metal</u> to put around her luggage. ....

f In the 1800s, a man or woman wore a <u>long dress</u> when he or she went to bed.
....

g The Yolland family live in a <u>small house</u> in a fishing village. ....

h Rachel is angry about losing her diamond and when she wants to say something she <u>comes suddenly</u> out of her room. ....

i The police look around the house trying to find <u>things that will help them to understand the mystery</u>. ....

j Rachel <u>disagrees strongly</u> when Sergeant Cuff wants to look at everyone's clothes to try and find the paint mark. ....

k Rachel's behaviour was <u>showing that she had done something bad</u>. ....

GUESS WHAT

What do you think happens in the next chapter? Complete the sentences with the names.

Rachel   Rosanna   Murthwaite   Franklin   Betteredge

a .... leaves Lady Verinder's house.

b .... wants to tell Franklin something.

c .... tells Sergeant Cuff that the Indians did not steal the Moonstone.

d Sergeant Cuff suspects that .... has the diamond.

e .... dies at the Shivering Sand.

Chapter 4

Death at the Shivering Sand

It had rained in the night, and that morning there was a strong wind and there were dark clouds in the sky. Sergeant Cuff planned to go to Frizinghall to continue his investigation there. When he walked out of the house, Betteredge and Franklin were in the garden. Although Franklin had been happy to see Cuff arrive the day before, he was now worried that the sergeant suspected that Rachel herself had hidden the diamond somewhere.

'Is it true that Rosanna Spearman came to speak to you last night?' asked Sergeant Cuff.

'I have nothing to say,' replied Franklin.

Just then, Rosanna Spearman and Penelope walked into the garden, near enough to hear the conversation.

'If you have Rosanna's interests at heart, Mr Franklin, you will explain everything,' continued Cuff.

'I have no interest at all in Rosanna Spearman,' replied Franklin coldly.

'I see,' said Sergeant Cuff, and he walked on to Frizinghall.

❖

Not long after the rest of the family had finished breakfast, Penelope came to tell her father some worrying news.

'I'm afraid, Father,' she explained, 'that Mr Franklin's unkind words have hurt Rosanna deeply. She has become very quiet and is working like a woman in a dream.'

Betteredge, who always felt sorry for Rosanna, went to talk to her. He explained that Franklin had spoken unkindly because he was angry with the sergeant. Rosanna said that she understood, but she still looked miserable.

'Is there something you want to tell me?' asked Betteredge.

'No,' replied Rosanna. 'But there is something I want to tell Mr Franklin.'

'Mr Franklin has gone for a walk,' said Betteredge.

'It doesn't matter, then. I won't trouble Mr Franklin today.' answered Rosanna.

Betteredge wanted to call the doctor to see Rosanna, but Dr Candy had caught a bad cold after Rachel's birthday party. He then went to talk to Lady Verinder, but she was busy helping Rachel to prepare her luggage. Rachel was very troubled about the lost diamond and she had decided to go and stay with her aunt and uncle – Godfrey Ablewhite's parents – in Frizinghall.

Just before two o'clock, Sergeant Cuff returned from Frizinghall. He had spoken to Mr Murthwaite about the dancers. Murthwaite was sure that the Indians had not stolen the diamond.

'But they are still looking for it,' warned Murthwaite. 'And they are clever enough to be able to find it!'

Then, Sergeant Cuff had asked about Rosanna Spearman. He found out that she had been to a shop on Thursday afternoon (the afternoon when she had pretended to be ill) and had bought some **cloth** – the kind of cloth that people use to make nightgowns.

❖

At two o'clock Rachel came downstairs. She was wearing a soft yellow dress and jacket, and a hat. She usually looked gentle, but now her eyes shone **fiercely**. She got into the **carriage**, while Lady Verinder, Sergeant Cuff and the servants stood at the door. Just then, Franklin ran up.

'Goodbye, Rachel,' he shouted after her.

cloth clothes are made from this

fiercely strongly and violently

carriage an old kind of car that horses pull

Her eyes shone fiercely.

23

'Drive on!' said Rachel to the driver, and she did not even turn to look at Franklin as she left.

Although Franklin and Rachel had been such good friends, she refused, in front of everyone, to say goodbye to him. Franklin was deeply hurt.

Sergeant Cuff was now sure that Rachel had the Moonstone with her, and he went quickly to question Rosanna Spearman. But Rosanna had disappeared.

❖

About an hour before, one of the servants had seen Rosanna; she was running towards the Shivering Sand. Sergeant Cuff and Betteredge ran to find her as fast as they could. As they got nearer to the beach, the clouds grew darker and it started to rain. They saw Rosanna's small **footprints** going into the sand, but Betteredge and Cuff could go no further. This was the Shivering Sand; if anyone stepped into that part of the beach, the sand pulled them down within minutes. The sea was coming in quickly. There was no escape.

'She has killed herself!' cried Betteredge, as he remembered Rosanna's sad face earlier that morning.

'What do you mean?' asked Cuff. 'We must save her!'

'Oh no, Sergeant Cuff. What the Sand gets, the Sand keeps.'

Betteredge and Cuff returned to the house in silence. They found a note in Rosanna's room.

Forgive me, Mr Betteredge.
I have lived and died grateful for your kindness.
Rosanna

When Lady Verinder heard the news, she called Sergeant Cuff to her room immediately.

'Why did Rosanna take her own life?' she asked him.

'Rosanna didn't steal the diamond, but she was worried about another person – your daughter! I suspect that Rachel has taken

footprint the hole that someone's foot makes in soft ground when they walk

24

her own diamond and that she now has the Moonstone with her.'

'Sergeant Cuff, as Rachel's mother, I must tell you that you are wrong about her.'

'Madam, please think about the facts more carefully. Miss Rachel refused to have her clothes examined; she was clearly angry with Mr Franklin today because he is the person who has helped most in this investigation; and finally, I think that she asked Rosanna Spearman to help her. Rosanna was once a thief and she knew jewellers in London who could buy a jewel like the Moonstone. Miss Rachel needed Rosanna to help her sell the diamond.'

Lady Verinder listened silently. Then after a moment she said: 'I will go to Rachel and tell her about Rosanna's death. I'm sure that she will tell me the **truth**.'

And Lady Verinder left immediately for Frizinghall.

Later that evening, a letter from Lady Verinder arrived for Sergeant Cuff.

> *Rachel told me – I feel truthfully – that she has not seen the diamond since she put it in the cabinet on the night of her birthday, and that she never spoke to Rosanna Spearman about the diamond.*

With the letter came a **cheque** to pay Sergeant Cuff. Cuff prepared to go back to London that evening.

Franklin also received a letter from Lady Verinder. It said that although she was very grateful for all Franklin's help, she felt it was better if he didn't try to see Rachel again for some time.

'When I came here with that diamond, this was the happiest house in England,' thought Franklin. 'And now the mystery of the jewel has destroyed the happiness of this family. The Moonstone has indeed brought the revenge that Colonel Herncastle was looking for.'

truth what is true

cheque a piece of paper from a bank that promises to pay money to someone

READING CHECK

1 Correct seven more mistakes in the chapter summary.

The next morning, Rosanna Spearman goes into the garden with ~~Rachel~~ Penelope. She hears

Franklin Blake tell Sergeant Cuff and Betteredge that he's not interested in her. Rosanna

is deeply hurt by Franklin's words and she looks very happy all morning. Betteredge

comes to talk to Rosanna but she says that she wants to talk to Lady Verinder.

At two o'clock in the afternoon, Rachel leaves to go and stay with her cousin Godfrey

in Frizinghall. After she has left, Sergeant Cuff wants to speak to Rosanna. He and

Betteredge follow her to the Yollands' cottage. But they are too late. Rosanna has

already walked onto the dangerous path and it has pulled her under. Sergeant Cuff and

Betteredge can't forgive her. 'She has killed herself,' says Sergeant Cuff.

2 Use the correct names to complete Sergeant Cuff's notes about the investigation.

  a This morning I went to ...Frizinghall... to continue my investigations.

  b Before leaving, I asked Franklin Blake about his conversation with ....

  c I spoke to Mr .... about the three Indian dancers.

  d I found out that .... pretended to be ill and went to Frizinghall to do some
     shopping.

  e When Miss Rachel left this afternoon, she refused to say goodbye to ....

  f I think that Rosanna Spearman killed herself because she was helping ....
     to hide the Moonstone.

  g .... has gone to Frizinghall to tell Rachel about Rosanna's death.

WORD WORK

Find the words in the beach to complete the sentences.

a He is very honest and always tells the ......truth...... .

b You can pay by credit card or by .... if you want.

c We went to a large shop to buy some .... to make covers for the armchairs.

d Before people had cars, they travelled by horse and ....

e Robinson Crusoe was alone on his island until one day he discovered a .... in the sand.

f The army fought .... and won the battle.

GUESS WHAT

Match the sentence halves to find out what happens in the next chapter.

a Franklin decides to . . .

b Lady Verinder takes Rachel to London to . . .

c Godfrey Ablewhite goes to . . .

d Rachel agrees to . . .

e Rachel wants Godfrey to . . .

f Lady Verinder calls the family lawyer to . . .

1 write her will.

2 go abroad.

3 tell her about an attack by three Indians.

4 forget about the diamond.

5 marry Godfrey.

6 visit Rachel and Lady Verinder in London.

Chapter 5

The mystery moves to London

Franklin left Yorkshire that evening and went back to London. He couldn't stop thinking about Rachel, or the mystery of the Moonstone. He decided to go abroad and try to forget everything.

Lady Verinder also wanted to help her daughter forget about the trouble that the diamond had brought, and decided to take Rachel to their house in London. Penelope prepared their luggage and went with them.

Sergeant Cuff had also returned to London. Although Lady Verinder had asked him not to investigate the diamond mystery any more, he read an **article** in the newspaper a few days later with great interest.

30th June 1848

Yesterday afternoon, two gentlemen became **victims** of a strange attack. One gentleman was Mr Septimus Luker, a jeweller from Lambeth, and the other was Mr Godfrey Ablewhite. The gentlemen were seen leaving a bank in Lombard Street at the same time. Later that afternoon, Mr Ablewhite received a letter which told him to go to a house in Northumberland Street. When he entered the house, Mr Ablewhite noticed a small statue of an Indian god on the table. He was led into a room where three men with dark skins were waiting. Suddenly, from behind, Mr Ablewhite felt an arm around his neck and he was thrown to the floor. The attackers searched Mr Ablewhite very carefully, but they did not find what they were looking for, and quickly left the house.

A short while later, the same thing happened to Mr Luker at a house in Alfred Place, near Tottenham Court Road. Mr Luker was thrown to the floor, tied up, and searched. Three dark-skinned men were seen leaving the house. After the attack Mr Luker noticed that a bank **receipt** was missing from his pocket. The receipt was for a valuable jewel that Mr Luker had left at the bank that morning. Mr Luker hurried to the bank, but the attackers had not yet been there, and the jewel was safe.

article a piece of writing in a newspaper

victim someone who is hurt

receipt a piece of paper that says that something belongs to you

People started talking about the news, and soon there were **rumours** all around London that the attacks were something to do with the missing Moonstone diamond. A few days later Godfrey Ablewhite went to visit Lady Verinder and Rachel at their house in Montague Street.

'Please don't worry about me,' he said charmingly, when they asked him about the attack. 'It was just a mistake; they thought I was another man.'

'But the three Indian men that attacked you – were they the same men that came to the house on the evening of my birthday party?' asked Rachel quickly.

'My dear Rachel, it happened so quickly, I did not see their faces well enough to say,' he replied calmly.

'And what about Mr Luker's bank receipt? People say it was for a valuable jewel,' continued Rachel. 'A jewel like the Moonstone!'

Godfrey began to look very uncomfortable but Rachel became more excited.

'And they say that you, Godfrey, sold it to Mr Luker!'

Lady Verinder couldn't **believe** what her daughter was saying.

Rachel jumped up from her chair and **declared**: 'I know the hand that took the Moonstone, and I know that you are **innocent**, Godfrey! I will write to the newspapers and tell them myself!'

Just then, there was a knock at the door. Some friends had arrived to take Rachel out for the day. Rachel kissed her mother, said goodbye to Godfrey, and left.

❖

Later that afternoon, Lady Verinder had another visitor. It was Mr Bruff, the family lawyer. Since they had moved to London, Lady Verinder had been unwell. Her doctor had told her that she was seriously ill. She knew that she did not have long to live, so she had called Mr Bruff to help her write her will. Mr Bruff was also **anxious** to talk to Lady Verinder about another matter.

'Have you heard what people are saying about your nephew,

rumour a story that may not be true, but that people like to tell

believe to feel sure that something is true

declare to say something that you think is important

innocent having done nothing wrong

anxious worried and excited

Godfrey Ablewhite?' Mr Bruff asked. 'I'm afraid that, since the attack by the Indians, there are rumours that he stole the diamond.'

'What a stupid idea!' replied Lady Verinder. 'Sergeant Cuff was sure that my own daughter had taken the diamond and hidden it! This terrible Moonstone is destroying my family.'

'Lady Verinder, I have known your family for a long time. Miss Rachel is the most honest young lady that I have ever met. She could not possibly do such a thing – but I'm not so sure about Godfrey Ablewhite . . .'

'I must tell you, Mr Bruff, that earlier today Rachel declared that Godfrey was innocent.'

'Well, if Rachel says that he is innocent, then I believe her. But then who . . . ?'

Mr Bruff and Lady Verinder did not want to think about the mystery any more, and they turned to the matter of the will.

❖

The next day Rachel again went out with her friends. Lady Verinder was not feeling well and stayed at home to rest, and Godfrey Ablewhite went out with Rachel instead of her. When they got back home, Godfrey wanted to talk to Rachel, and so they went to the library. There Godfrey sat down opposite Rachel.

'Rachel,' he declared, 'I am hopelessly in love with you!'

'But Godfrey,' Rachel protested, 'didn't we agree on the day of my birthday party to be friends and no more?'

'I have tried, Rachel,' Godfrey replied. 'But my feelings for you have not changed.'

'I have something to tell you, Godfrey, that will make you change your mind. I was in love with another man, but he **betrayed** me and I will never, never see him again!'

Rachel spoke angrily, and burst into tears. But when Godfrey realised how honest Rachel was, he told her that he loved her even more. He **knelt** down in front of her.

'Dearest Rachel,' Godfrey said gently, 'there is a way to forget the

betray to do something bad against someone who is your friend

kneel (*past* **knelt**) to rest on your knees

man that betrayed you. Please marry me!'

Rachel protested, but Godfrey went on asking her to marry him. He was a very good speaker and finally Rachel agreed. Just then, they heard a servant shouting; 'Miss Rachel, come quickly! Your mother has fallen ill.'

At once Rachel ran to her mother's room and threw her arms around Lady Verinder. But she was already dead.

'Please marry me!'

READING CHECK

Match the sentences with the people.

> Franklin Lady Verinder Rachel Sergeant Cuff
>
> Mr Luker Godfrey Ablewhite Mr Bruff

a .....Franklin..... decides to go abroad.

b .... and .... move to their house in London.

c .... reads an interesting article in the newspaper.

d .... and .... are attacked by dark-skinned strangers.

e .... has left a valuable jewel at the bank.

f .... goes to visit Lady Verinder and Rachel at their house in Montague Stree

g .... says that Godfrey did not steal the Moonstone.

h .... comes to help Lady Verinder write her will.

i .... asks Rachel to marry him.

j .... dies.

WORD WORK

Use the definitions to complete the crossword.

Down

1 you do this to a friend when you promise to keep a secret, and then you tell the secret to another person

2 you feel this when you are waiting for your exam results

4 to speak in a way when you have something important to say and you want everyone to hear you

6 a piece of writing in a newspaper is called this

9 a person that is hurt by an accident or by an attack

Across

3 you are this when other people think you have done something wrong, but you have not done it

5 you get one when you buy something in a shop, to show that you have paid for it

7 this is a story about people that we like to tell, though it may not be true

8 you do this when you are sure that what someone says is true

10 to go on the floor on your knees

¹B
E
T
R
A
Y

GUESS WHAT

What do you think happens in the next chapter? Tick the boxes.

a After her mother's death, Rachel . . .
  1 ☐ goes to live with her aunt and uncle in Frizinghall.
  2 ☐ lives alone in the house in Yorkshire.
  3 ☐ goes to India.

b Mr Bruff is surprised when . . .
  1 ☐ Lady Verinder leaves everything to Rachel in her will.
  2 ☐ Rachel changes her mind about getting married.
  3 ☐ an Indian gentleman comes to his office to borrow money.

c At dinner Mr Bruff meets . . .
  1 ☐ Mr Murthwaite.
  2 ☐ Godfrey Ablewhite.
  3 ☐ Franklin Blake.

d Mr Murthwaite believes that . . .
  1 ☐ Rachel knows where the Moonstone is.
  2 ☐ someone gave the Moonstone to Mr Luker.
  3 ☐ the Indians will never find the Moonstone.

e Godfrey Ablewhite goes to Mr Bruff's office to . . .
  1 ☐ borrow money.
  2 ☐ make a will.
  3 ☐ examine Lady Verinder's will.

Chapter 6

Unexpected news

Lady Verinder was **buried** at the small **cemetery** in the park of the house in Yorkshire. In her will she had left everything to Rachel, her only daughter. She had also asked her brother, Old Mr Ablewhite, Rachel's uncle in Frizinghall, to look after Rachel either until she reached the age of twenty-one, or until she got married. Old Mr Ablewhite knew that Rachel was **engaged to** his son, so he was careful to make sure that Rachel was made as comfortable as possible.

❖

About a week after Rachel had left London to go back to Yorkshire, an **unexpected** visitor arrived at Mr Bruff's office. The man was tall and thin, very well-dressed in a fine suit, and dark-skinned. Mr Bruff did not usually agree to meet strangers in his office, but he supposed that the man was an Indian, and that he might know something about the Moonstone. (Mr Bruff had known the Moonstone for a long time; he had been Colonel Herncastle's lawyer, and Bruff had arranged the Colonel's will which had left the diamond to Rachel.)

'I have come, sir,' began the Indian gentleman very politely, 'to ask you to lend me some money. Please keep this jewel box until I pay back the **debt**.'

The Indian placed a small, black box covered in jewels on the desk. It was worth a lot of money.

'I'm afraid, sir,' replied Mr Bruff, 'that lending money is not my business. You need to visit a jeweller, like Mr Luker. He can lend you money for this jewel box.'

'I see,' said the Indian gentleman. 'Then I am very sorry to trouble you. But before I go, could I ask just one question? In this country, if you borrow money, when must you pay back the debt?'

'The law in this country says that you must pay back your debt in one year.'

bury to put a dead person under the ground

cemetery a place where dead people are put under the ground

engaged to going to marry

unexpected not waited for

debt money that you must pay back to someone

'Thank you very much for your help,' said the Indian gentleman, and he **bowed** politely and left.

That evening, Mr Bruff went to a dinner party. One of the guests at the party was Mr Murthwaite, the famous Indian traveller. After dinner, Mr Bruff was sitting next to Murthwaite, and he began talking about the strange visit to his office that afternoon.

'Mmm,' said Murthwaite when he heard the story. 'So the Moonstone is in London.'

'What do you mean?' asked Bruff. 'The Moonstone is missing! Everyone knows that!'

'Thank you very much for your help.'

bow to put down your head in front of someone important

'Let me tell you what I know about this dangerous jewel. A number of Indian priests have been following the Moonstone since it was taken from the Palace of Seringapatam in 1799. They have been in this country, and are waiting for their chance to take the diamond back to the statue of the Moon God, where it belongs. When Colonel Herncastle died and the diamond was taken to Yorkshire, this was the chance that the Indian priests were waiting for. Unfortunately for them, Franklin Blake changed his travel plans at the last moment, and the Indians lost their chance to attack Franklin and **recover** the diamond. But they saw the jewel on Rachel's dress at the birthday party, and waited for their next chance. And when did we next hear about the Indian gentlemen?' asked Murthwaite.

'The attack on Mr Luker and Godfrey Ablewhite,' answered Bruff.

'That's right,' said Murthwaite. 'They followed the diamond back to London. Someone left it with Mr Luker and the Indians took a second chance to recover it. Luckily, Mr Luker had already put the diamond in the bank and it was safe. But you understand the Indian gentleman's question, don't you?' asked Murthwaite.

'Of course! I see now,' answered Bruff. 'Someone borrowed money from Mr Luker, and gave him the diamond to keep until the debt is paid back. The person must pay back the debt in a year, and at that time Mr Luker will give back the diamond.'

'And that will be the Indian priests' third chance to recover the Moonstone,' warned Murthwaite.

❖

In her will, Lady Verinder had left Rachel a great **fortune**. But the will also said that Rachel could not sell any of the land or houses that Lady Verinder had left her; she could only live comfortably from a yearly **income** for the rest of her life.

Rachel was lonely without her mother, and, until she got married, she was living with her aunt and uncle in Frizinghall. Mrs Ablewhite saw how miserable Rachel was and took her to live

recover to take back something that belongs to you

fortune money, houses, and valuable things that make you a rich person

income money that you get every month, or every year

in Brighton, a seaside town not far from London.

Soon after Mrs Ablewhite and Rachel had arrived at the house in Brighton, they received a visit from Mr Bruff. That afternoon, Mr Bruff asked Rachel to take a walk along the beach with him. He had something to tell her.

'Rachel, I hear that you are engaged to Godfrey Ablewhite. Do you really love him?' asked Mr Bruff.

'I am marrying him because it is my only chance to find a little happiness in my life,' Rachel answered.

'And do you believe that Godfrey loves you?' he asked.

Rachel stopped. 'Mr Bruff, if you have something to tell me about Godfrey, then please say it!'

Mr Bruff explained that soon after Lady Verinder's death, Godfrey had visited his offices and had asked to examine Lady Verinder's will. Mr Bruff was worried that Godfrey was marrying Rachel only for her money. Rachel's face became white, and she held onto Mr Bruff's arm. Finally she said;

'I will talk to Godfrey myself. Thank you for what you have told me, Mr Bruff.'

The next day Godfey Ablewhite arrived from London. At once Rachel told him that she had changed her mind and no longer wished to marry him.

'I'm sorry Godfrey. I wanted to forget about the other man that I loved. This was not a good reason for agreeing to marry you. I made a mistake,' she explained.

But Godfrey did not protest. He accepted her change of heart immediately! At first Rachel was surprised by Godfrey's behaviour, and then she realised that he had indeed only been interested in her fortune. The fact that Rachel could not sell any of her houses or land meant that Godfrey could not get a large **sum** of money if he married her. Mr Bruff had been right! Godfrey had never really been in love with her.

Later that day, Rachel left the house in Brighton and went to live with Mr Bruff's family in London.

sum an amount of something

READING CHECK

Match the first and second parts of these sentences.

a Lady Verinder has asked . . .

b Mrs Ablewhite takes . . .

c An Indian gentleman asks . . .

d Mr Bruff talks to . . .

e Mr Murthwaite warns . . .

f Mr Bruff tells . . .

g Rachel tells . . .

h Godfrey accepts . . .

1 Mr Murthwaite about the Moonstone at a dinner party.

2 Godfrey that she doesn't want to marry him.

3 her brother to look after Rachel until she gets married.

4 Mr Bruff to lend him money.

5 Rachel something important about Godfrey Ablewhite.

6 that the Indians will try to get the Moonstone again next year.

7 Rachel's change of heart without protesting.

8 Rachel to live in Brighton.

WORD WORK

Correct the boxed words in the sentences. They all come from Chapter 6.

a When Lady Verinder dies, she leaves a great fortress to Rachel. ..fortune...

b Rachel goes back to the house in Yorkshire to berry her mother, but she doesn't want to live there alone. ....

c Lady Verinder's will gives Rachel an inform, so she has enough money to live comfortably. ....

d Mr Bruff receives an unrespected visit from an Indian gentleman. ....

e The Indian gentleman vows politely before leaving the room. ....

f The Indians have already had two chances to recorder the Moonstone, but they were unsuccessful. ....

g Mr Luker is keeping a valuable jewel until someone pays back the deft. ....

h Rachel is enraged to Godfrey Ablewhite, but she changes her mind. ....

i A ceremony is a place where dead people are buried. ....

j The Moonstone is worth a large sun of money. ....

GUESS WHAT

**In the next chapter Franklin comes back to England.
What do you think he does? Tick or cross the boxes.**

a He goes to live with Mr Bruff. ☐

b He goes back to the house in Yorkshire. ☐

c He asks Rachel to marry him. ☐

d He reads a letter from Rosanna Spearman. ☐

e He finds the nightgown with the paint smear. ☐

f He finds the Moonstone. ☐

Chapter 7

An important discovery

In the spring of 1849, Franklin Blake was still travelling abroad. Although he had already been away for nine months, he was still not able to forget about Rachel. Then one day, Franklin received news that his father had died. A letter from Mr Bruff told him that he had **inherited** a great fortune and asked him to come home immediately.

As Franklin got nearer and nearer to England, he thought about seeing Rachel again. When he met Mr Bruff in London, Franklin's first question was about her. Mr Bruff gave him Rachel's address, and half an hour later Franklin was knocking at her door.

'Miss Rachel is not at home,' said the servant. Although Franklin visited Rachel again and again, and wrote letters to her, she wanted nothing to do with him. Franklin was sure that her silence was because of the Moonstone mystery. Franklin was determined to find out the truth, and so he took the next train to Yorkshire.

❖

When Franklin arrived at the house in Yorkshire, the old servant Betteredge was happy, but surprised, to see him.

'What has brought you here, Mr Franklin?' he asked.

'The same as brought me here almost a year ago; the Moonstone,' answered Franklin.

'That Moonstone has brought nothing but trouble. It's better to leave it alone.'

'Do you remember how angry Rachel was when she left this house? She behaved so unkindly to me and refused to say goodbye. Well, she is still angry with me. I'm going to **solve** the mystery, once and for all. Perhaps then she will speak to me again.'

Betteredge had watched Rachel and Franklin become good friends during the month before the birthday party, and many of the servants had hoped at that time to see them become man and

inherit to receive a fortune when your parents die

solve to find the answer to a mystery

wife. Betteredge could see now that Franklin was still in love with Rachel a year later.

'Tell me Betteredge, did anything happen after I left the house?' asked Franklin excitedly.

'Well, the day after you left, I received a visit from **Limping** Lucy, the daughter of Yolland the fisherman. She brought a letter for you. Do you remember the servant Rosanna Spearman?' asked Betteredge.

'Of course! She was the poor woman who took her life at the Shivering Sand,' replied Franklin.

'That's right,' continued Betteredge. 'Well, a few days before that, she visited the Yollands' cottage and wrote a letter to you. She gave the letter to her only friend, Limping Lucy, and asked her to **deliver** it to you in person. You had already gone back to London, and Lucy refused to give the letter to me, so she still has it now.'

'A letter from Rosanna Spearman? I remember that she behaved very strangely; I thought that she wanted to tell me something. Perhaps she wrote about it in the letter . . .'

First thing the next morning, the two men walked to the fisherman's cottage. When they stepped into Mrs Yolland's kitchen, they found a young woman there. She was small and thin, with dark wild hair and fierce eyes. She stared angrily at Franklin, and limped across the kitchen towards them.

'This is Mr Franklin Blake,' Betteredge told Lucy. 'You have a letter from Rosanna for him.'

Without a word, Lucy fetched the letter and took Franklin outside. They walked a little way from the cottage and stopped behind some boats.

'So you are Rosanna's murderer!' she said to him **boldly**.

'What *do* you mean?' asked Franklin angrily.

'Rosanna told me, "There are men who are worth dying for and Franklin Blake is one of them!" She took care of you and worried about you, but you never even noticed her. She was my dearest

limp to walk unevenly because you have a bad leg

deliver to give a letter to someone

boldly bravely

friend and you took her away from me! Take your letter. I hope that I never see you again.'

She threw the letter at Franklin and limped away noisily. Franklin opened Rosanna's letter and read it at once. It was a page of **instructions**:

> Go to the Shivering Sand when the sea is low. Walk out to sea along the low rocks on the far side of the beach. When you can see the Yollands' cottage at the other side of the Shivering Sand, then lie down on the rocks and feel in the sand at the edge of the rocks. You will find a chain that is tied to the rocks. Pull the chain out of the sand.

Franklin gave the message to Betteredge to read.

'So Rosanna *was* hiding something after all,' said Betteredge, 'The sea is going out now. Let's go straight to the Shivering Sand.'

They soon reached the lonely beach. It was a fine spring day and the wet sand shone in the sunlight. The sea was very low now. Carefully Franklin walked along the rocks and followed Rosanna's instructions. He knelt down and carefully felt at the edge of the rocks for the chain. As Franklin looked across the beach, he thought he could see Rosanna's ghost coming out of the sand to help him. He quickly searched for the chain and put his hand into the low water. He felt the chain and pulled it; a small black box appeared.

Franklin ran back to Betteredge with the box and they opened it at once. Inside they found a letter and a man's nightgown. When they examined the nightgown more carefully, they found some paint on it. They remembered Sergeant Cuff's words; 'When you find the clothes that made the paint smear, you can find the diamond.'

instructions
words that tell
you what to do

They looked inside the nightgown to find who it belonged to. They saw the letters 'F.B.' Franklin had indeed discovered the truth about the Moonstone; although he did not remember the fact, he himself seemed to be the thief!

❖

Later, back at the house, Franklin and Betteredge tried to understand what they had found.

'I am innocent,' said Franklin. 'I did not take the diamond, but the **evidence points** to me!'

Betteredge poured another glass of brandy and told Franklin to read the letter that they had found in the small black box.

Dear Sir,   Friday, 23rd June 1848

When you read these words, I will be dead. You may wonder why I have behaved so strangely. It is because I love you. I know that you are in love with Miss Rachel. Every day I have hoped that you will notice me, but now I realize that my love for you is hopeless.

And with this letter you will find your nightgown. The day that the diamond went missing, I followed the other servants to Miss Rachel's room to **complain** to Detective Seagrave. It was then that he pointed to the smear in the paint on Miss Rachel's door. Afterwards I went to do my work. I went to your room to make your bed and put away your nightgown. To my great surprise I discovered a paint smear on your nightgown! When I thought that you had stolen the diamond, my feelings for you grew stronger; you were a thief like me. And if you wanted to sell the diamond and get money, then I could help you. I could take you to a man in London that buys such valuable jewels . . .

evidence a piece of information that helps you to find the truth about a mystery or a crime

point to show where something is with your finger

complain to say that you are unhappy or angry about something

quicksand a kind of sand that is dangerous because it pulls you down into it

wrinkled with many lines on your skin

list a lot of names that you write one after the other

The letter continued to explain how, to save Franklin, Rosanna had bought cloth and made a new nightgown to replace the one with the paint smear on it, and how she had hidden the evidence in the **quicksand** of the Shivering Sand.

When Franklin and Betteredge finished reading the letter, they were both deep in thought. Suddenly there was a knock at the door. A strange-looking man came in. He had a dark, **wrinkled** face, and curly hair, which was black on top, and very white at the sides of his head. His soft brown eyes looked towards Franklin, who was staring rudely back at him.

'I'm sorry. I had no idea that you were busy, Mr Betteredge. Here's the **list** of sick people for next week,' he said.

And the man left the room as suddenly as he had entered.

'Who was that?!' asked Franklin.

'That's Dr Candy's assistant,' explained Betteredge. 'The doctor

'Here's the list of sick people for next week.'

fell ill after Rachel's birthday party, and he has not yet recovered from his illness. His assistant does all his work now. Every week he brings me a list of the sick people in Frizinghall, and we send wine and food to them.'

'And what is the man's name?' asked Franklin.

'Ezra Jennings – an **ugly** name for an ugly man!'

❖

Franklin decided to take the letter and the nightgown to Mr Bruff, and to ask for his advice. On the way to the station, Franklin asked Betteredge, 'Was I drunk on the night of Rachel's birthday?'

'Of course not! In fact, you looked miserable and I took you a glass of brandy and water before you went to bed.'

'And Betteredge, have you ever seen me sleep-walking?'

'Sleep-walking? No never!' the old servant replied. 'And, sir, suppose that you did take the diamond, then how is it in London now?'

At the station, Franklin was just about to get on the train for London, when he looked over to the small shop. There was that strange man, Ezra Jennings, again. He was talking to someone, but he looked up and saw Franklin getting on the train.

When Franklin arrived back in London, he went straight to Mr Bruff's house and showed him the letter and the nightgown. After he had examined them carefully, Mr Bruff said:

'Franklin, this is a very serious matter. Now I understand Rachel's behaviour. She thinks that you stole her diamond. The next step in this investigation is to speak to Rachel.'

'I want to speak to her myself, then,' said Franklin.

'Are you sure?' asked Mr Bruff. 'You told me that Rachel has refused to meet you.'

'Mr Bruff, please invite Rachel to your home tomorrow. I will come here at three o'clock to meet her, but don't tell her that I am coming. Give me a key so that I can enter your house through the garden.'

Mr Bruff agreed to the plan.

ugly not beautiful

READING CHECK

Correct the mistakes in these sentences.

father

a Franklin is travelling abroad when he receives a letter saying that his ~~uncle~~ has died.

b Rachel refuses to see Franklin because she is happy with him.

c Betteredge tells Franklin that Rosanna Spearman has been keeping a letter for him.

d Franklin follows the instructions in Rosanna's letter and finds the Moonstone.

e Franklin remembers going into Rachel's sitting room and taking the Moonstone.

f When Betteredge and Franklin finish reading Rosanna's letter, Dr Candy comes into the room.

g Mr Bruff understands Rachel's behaviour; she thinks that Franklin sold her diamond.

h Mr Bruff agrees to invite Rachel to his house because Betteredge needs to speak to her.

WORD WORK

Use the words round the statue to complete the sentences on page 47.

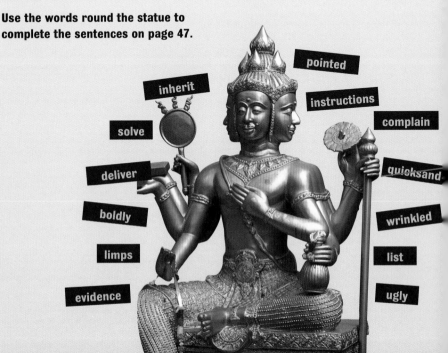

pointed

inherit

instructions

solve

complain

deliver

quicksand

boldly

wrinkled

limps

list

evidence

ugly

a Don't go near that part of the beach; if you walk across there, the .quicksand. pulls you down in minutes.

b The colonel is angry about his son's marriage to the housemaid; he has re-written his will and his son isn't going to .... anything.

c Her leg was badly hurt in a car accident two years ago; she still ....

d You can order your shopping on your computer and the supermarket will .... it to your house the same day.

e In the middle of the lesson, one fearless student stood up and told the teacher .... that she had made a mistake.

f The nightgown with a paint smear on it is important .... to help .... the Moonstone mystery; it shows who took the Moonstone.

g Before you start using the camera, please read the .... carefully.

h Some tourists wanted to go to the London Eye, but they didn't understand English so we .... to show them the way.

i Have you seen the guest .... for the dinner party? There are fifty names on it!

j The cakes weren't very good and the coffee was cold, but we couldn't .... because it was my friend's restaurant.

k This dress is not very pretty; it makes me look really ....!

l After many years of working outside, the farmer's face was brown and............... .

GUESS WHAT

Make four sentences with these phrases and find out what happens in the next chapter.

a Rachel	**e** suggests	**i** who wants to tell him something.
b Franklin	**f** goes to visit Dr Candy	
c Ezra Jennings	**g** tells Franklin who	**j** how to prove Franklin's innocence.
d Ezra Jennings	**h** explains what	**k** took the diamond.
		l Dr Candy said during his fever.

Chapter 8

An experiment

At three o'clock the next afternoon, Franklin opened the door into Mr Bruff's garden. As he walked towards the house, he could hear Rachel playing the piano. Franklin went into the house, and made his way to the music room. He stood outside the room for a few moments before he opened the door.

When Rachel saw Franklin she stopped playing the piano and stood up. Rachel and Franklin looked at each other across the room, and for a few minutes they stood still.

'Rachel,' said Franklin softly.

Rachel slowly walked towards Franklin. He looked at her beautiful face and shining bright eyes. He took her in his arms and **kissed** her. At first Rachel accepted his kisses, but then she pushed him away angrily.

'Is this the behaviour of a gentleman?' she asked angrily. 'Why do you come here secretly and make me kiss you? You were once very dear to me, but now-'

kiss to touch
lovingly with your
mouth

She turned away and began to cry.

'Rachel, please listen. Let me explain,' said Franklin gently. He wanted to tell her about his discovery of the nightgown and about Rosanna Spearman's letter.

'There is nothing to explain,' cried Rachel between her **tears**. 'I saw you take my diamond with my own eyes!'

'Please Rachel, you must believe me! I am innocent. I do not remember taking the diamond. You must tell me everything that happened that night.'

Rachel had kept her secret for a long time and it was hard for her to speak about what had happened.

'At about twelve o'clock, after we had said goodnight, I went to bed. But I couldn't sleep and I got up to get a book from my sitting room. I opened my bedroom door and heard a noise outside. Then I saw a light under the sitting room door, and I blew out my **candle**. The door opened and I saw YOU! The light from your candle clearly showed me your face. I remember your eyes – they were brighter than usual. You walked straight to the cabinet and you took the Moonstone. You held it in your right hand, you

'You walked straight to the cabinet and you took the Moonstone.'

tear water that comes from your eye when you cry

candle it burns and gives light; in the past people used them to see at night

stopped to think for a few moments, and then you left the room with the diamond.'

Franklin was silent. He was indeed the person who had stolen the jewel. After a while Franklin asked, 'Why didn't you tell us about this? Why did you keep it secret?'

'What a stupid question!' said Rachel angrily. 'How can I tell everyone that the man I love is a thief? I didn't tell anyone but I wrote you a letter. I offered to help you if you needed money, and I asked you to return the diamond. But you never got that letter because I destroyed it when you went to fetch the police. You pretended to everyone that you wanted to help me find the jewel that you had stolen!'

Franklin couldn't listen any more.

'Rachel, I will **prove** that I am innocent. I will not see you again until I can prove my **innocence**.'

Franklin left, and tears filled Rachel's eyes once more when she thought of never seeing Franklin again.

❖

That evening, Mr Bruff came to see Franklin.

'Well,' said Mr Bruff, when Franklin had finished telling him Rachel's story, 'we have discovered who took the diamond. But we have not yet found the Moonstone itself. How did it get to London, and who borrowed money from Mr Luker?'

The person who had borrowed money from Mr Luker had to pay back the debt at the end of June, and at the same time Mr Luker had to return the diamond to this person. Mr Bruff had a plan.

'At the end of the month I will send someone to watch the bank and tell us when Mr Luker goes to fetch the Moonstone,' explained Mr Bruff. 'If we can discover who borrowed Mr Luker's money, I'm sure that we can find the person who took the diamond.'

'But it's nearly two weeks until the end of the month. I can't wait until then,' said Franklin. 'We need Sergeant Cuff's help.'

The next morning Franklin went to find Sergeant Cuff. The detective had stopped working with the police, and now he was

prove to make people see that something is true

innocence when you have not done anything wrong

living in a cottage in the country. But when Franklin got there the sergeant was not at home. He was away in Ireland. So Franklin left a letter which told him that there was news about the Moonstone.

When Franklin got back to London, a letter from Betteredge was waiting. It said that Dr Candy wanted to speak to Franklin the next time he came to Frizinghall. Franklin prepared to go to Yorkshire immediately. Dr Candy had been a guest at Rachel's birthday dinner and Franklin hoped that he remembered something. Franklin needed any clue to help him.

Before leaving, Franklin called on Godfrey Ablewhite. Godfrey had also been a guest at the birthday dinner, and Franklin wanted to ask him for information, too. But Godfrey had left the day before to go travelling in Europe.

❖

So Franklin travelled to Yorkshire and went to visit Dr Candy. Franklin was surprised to see how Dr Candy had changed. The doctor's illness had turned his hair grey, and his face had become wrinkled. But the worst thing about the illness was that Dr Candy had lost his **memory**.

'Dr Candy, you sent a message to say that you had something to tell me,' began Franklin.

'Oh yes! I sent you a message,' said Dr Candy. 'That's right.'

'Was it something to do with Miss Verinder's birthday dinner?' asked Franklin.

'That's it! The birthday dinner! It was a very pleasant dinner, wasn't it?' said Dr Candy.

The conversation continued, but Dr Candy couldn't remember what he wanted to tell Franklin. Franklin decided to leave, and he went to the door. At the door he met Ezra Jennings, who was on his way out to see one of Dr Candy's patients. He was taking the same road as Franklin, so they walked together. Ezra spoke about Dr Candy's illness. 'After the birthday dinner, Dr Candy went home in the rain, and got very wet. Later he caught a **fever**, Mr Franklin, and nearly died. I took care of him, and spent many

memory what you remember

fever when you get very hot because you are ill

hours at his side. During the fever, Dr Candy spoke a lot, but it was difficult to understand what he was trying to say.'

'Did he say anything about the Moonstone?' asked Franklin.

'He said nothing about the Moonstone, Mr Franklin,' replied Ezra.

'And did he say my name, or talk about me?'

'Sir, I am Dr Candy's assistant. I'm not free to tell you what he said to me during a fever.'

'Ezra Jennings, I am in love with a woman. If I don't prove my innocence, I can never see her again. Please help me.'

Ezra Jennings had had a hard and miserable life. He too had once been in love, and he had a child that he could now never see. He looked at this young, fine-looking man, and felt sorry for him.

'You are in love. I see. Then, perhaps there is something that I can tell you. Come to Dr Candy's house this evening.'

❖

That evening, at Dr Candy's house, Franklin Blake and Ezra Jennings sat in a small room. Ezra asked Franklin to tell him about the **argument** with Dr Candy at dinner on the night of Rachel's birthday.

'I was not sleeping well at the time,' began Franklin, 'Because I had stopped smoking. Smoking helps me to calm down, but I stopped because Rachel didn't like the smell. When I spoke about this at the dinner table, Dr Candy told me that taking medicine could help me sleep. But I refused his medicine and said that I didn't believe it could help me or anyone.'

'And were you worried about the diamond that night?' asked Ezra.

'Yes, I heard Rachel's conversation with Lady Verinder about putting the diamond in the cabinet. I thought that it wasn't safe to leave it there.'

'Then, I think that I can explain what happened that night,' said Ezra. 'This is what Dr Candy said during his fever. I wrote down his words. Here they are.'

argument an angry talk

Franklin read the page of notes that Ezra gave him:

Mr Franklin Blake ... can't sleep at night ... refuses my medicine ... at the dinner table ... says medicine doesn't work ... in front of all the guests ... I'll teach him what medicine can do ... Lady Verinder's medicine box ... one small spoon of **opium** ... he'll never know ... he'll drink the opium with brandy ... excellent sleep ... now Mr Blake ... what do you think about medicine?

'So you see, Dr Candy was angry with you about the argument during dinner, and he wanted to prove that medicine could work. He secretly put opium into the brandy and water that Betteredge brought you that night,' Ezra Jennings explained. 'You see, at first opium awakens the mind, but later it makes you very sleepy. You were worried about the diamond that night so in your sleep you went to take it in order to keep it safe. You didn't know what you were doing or where you put the diamond. There is only one way to prove your innocence Mr Blake – an experiment!'

Ezra Jennings wanted to give Franklin opium again and to watch what he did in his sleep. Ezra thought that Franklin perhaps could repeat what he had done when he took the diamond a year before, and that he could even show people where he had put the stolen diamond.

'But the diamond is in London,' Franklin protested. 'It can't possibly be in Lady Verinder's house.'

'Some people think that the Moonstone diamond is in London.

opium a drug; something that people take to make them feel calm or to stop pain

53

But how do we know that Mr Luker's 'valuable jewel' is indeed the Moonstone? I'm sure that this experiment will show us where it is.'

Franklin agreed to do the experiment. First he had to stop smoking again.

Ezra Jennings wrote to Rachel and asked her to let them use her house for the experiment. Rachel agreed immediately and asked if she could watch the experiment, too. Ezra secretly agreed to this, but he was careful not to tell Franklin about it. Then Ezra asked Betteredge to prepare the house in exactly the same way as it had been for the birthday party. Next he wrote to Mr Bruff in secret and asked him also to be a **witness** at the experiment.

Ten days later, everything was ready. And for ten days Franklin had slept badly. That evening, Franklin and Ezra went to the house and had dinner. Rachel and Mr Bruff arrived a little while later, but Ezra didn't tell Franklin about their arrival. Rachel was excited about the experiment and the chance to prove Franklin's innocence.

At eleven o'clock Franklin prepared to go to bed. Mr Bruff and Betteredge were both hiding in Franklin's bedroom. Rachel put a large stone in the Indian cabinet, and waited in her bedroom. Ezra Jennings poured a spoon of opium into a glass of brandy for Franklin to drink. Then Ezra sat down at the bottom of Franklin's bed and watched him.

Franklin lay down to sleep and didn't move for some time. Then suddenly he sat up in bed and started speaking to himself: 'Those Indians may be in the house.' Then Franklin lay down again. After another five minutes, he sat up and started talking again; 'The cabinet doesn't lock. Anybody can take it.' Next, Franklin stood up, took the candle by his bed, and walked to Rachel's room. Rachel was standing at the door of her bedroom. Ezra, Betteredge and Bruff followed Franklin quietly. Through the open door, they watched him go into Rachel's sitting room. Franklin went straight to the cabinet, picked up the stone, and turned round. He walked to the middle of the room and stopped.

witness
a person who sees something important and can say later that it happened

'Now, is he going to show us where he put the diamond?' thought Ezra Jennings.

They watched him go into Rachel's sitting room.

READING CHECK

Tick the best answers.

a Why is Rachel angry with Franklin?

1 ☐ Because he comes into the room while she is playing the piano.

2 ☑ Because he kisses her.

3 ☐ Because he is innocent.

b How does Rachel know that Franklin took the Moonstone from her cabinet?

1 ☐ She knows that Franklin is a thief.

2 ☐ Rosanna told her that he did it.

3 ☐ She saw him take it.

c What is Mr Bruff waiting for?

1 ☐ Mr Luker to fetch the diamond from the bank.

2 ☐ Sergeant Cuff to come back from holiday.

3 ☐ A letter from Dr Candy.

d What happened to Dr Candy after Rachel's birthday party?

1 ☐ He sent a message to Franklin.

2 ☐ He got wet and caught a fever.

3 ☐ He told a story to Ezra Jennings.

e Why did Dr Candy give opium to Franklin?

1 ☐ He wanted him to take the diamond.

2 ☐ He wanted to help him.

3 ☐ He wanted to show him that medicine works.

f What does Ezra Jennings want Franklin to do for the experiment?

1 ☐ To have a good sleep all night.

2 ☐ To show where the diamond is.

3 ☐ To take opium again.

g Who watches the experiment?

1 ☐ Rachel, Sergeant Cuff, Dr Candy and Ezra Jennings.

2 ☐ Rachel, Betteredge, Mr Bruff and Ezra Jennings.

3 ☐ Rachel, Betteredge, Godfrey Ablewhite, and Ezra Jennings.

h What did Franklin do after he took the opium?

1 ☐ He went to Rachel's cabinet.

2 ☐ He started talking to Ezra Jennings.

3 ☐ He went to sleep and didn't wake up.

WORD WORK

1 Find nine more words from Chapter 8 in the box of letters.

2 Use nine of the words from the wordsquare to complete Ezra Jennings's diary.

16th June, 1849
This evening, I tried to help Franklin Blake. With **(a)** ......tears...... *in his*
eyes he told me that he was in love with Miss Rachel, and I felt sorry for him.
I explained to him that Dr Candy had been angry about their
(b) .... *at the dinner party. Dr Candy put* **(c)** .... *in*
Franklin's brandy because he wanted to **(d)** .... *that medicine*
works. But after the party the poor doctor caught a **(e)** ...., *and*
lost his **(f)** .... *so he couldn't tell Franklin what he had done.*

26th June, 1849
The night of the experiment! Mr Bruff is here; I wrote to him secretly to ask
him to be a **(g)** .... *Miss Rachel is here too. She wants to watch*
the experiment, too, because she hopes that it will show Franklin's
(h) .... *She is waiting in her bedroom. There's a* **(i)** ....
beside Franklin's bed. Franklin has drunk the brandy and is lying down.

GUESS WHAT

What do you think happens in the next chapter? Tick four sentences.

a ☐ Franklin wakes up and remembers where he put the Moonstone.

b ☐ Everyone agrees that Franklin is innocent.

c ☐ Mr Luker goes to the bank in Lombard Street.

d ☐ Mr Luker gives the Moonstone to the three Indians.

e ☐ Sergeant Cuff comes back to continue the investigation.

f ☐ Godfrey Ablewhite takes the Moonstone to Amsterdam.

g ☐ Someone is killed by the three Indians.

Chapter 9

The truth

Franklin was standing in the middle of Rachel's sitting room, and he was holding the stone in his right hand. Ezra Jennings, Mr Bruff, Betteredge, and Rachel were watching him. What was his next move?

Suddenly Franklin dropped the stone out of his hand, went over to the sofa, lay down and went into a deep sleep.

'Now,' said Ezra Jennings quietly to everyone, 'does this experiment prove that Mr Franklin came here and took the Moonstone without knowing what he was doing?'

They all agreed that the experiment had proved Franklin's innocence.

'Mr Jennings,' continued Mr Bruff, 'We are very grateful to you. You have proved part of the mystery for us, but we still don't know what happened to the diamond after Franklin took it. Now I hope that I can solve the rest of the mystery. For the last two days someone has been watching the bank in Lombard Street. He's waiting to see when Mr Luker comes to fetch the jewel – which we all believe to be the Moonstone, Mr Jennings. I must get back to London first thing in the morning.'

They all went to bed, and left Franklin to sleep on the sofa in Rachel's sitting room. He slept deeply until eight o'clock in the morning, and when he opened his eyes, he saw Rachel kneeling beside him.

'You are innocent, Franklin,' she said. 'Now we can be together again.'

Again Franklin took Rachel in his arms and kissed her, but this time she did not push him away. After breakfast, Franklin and Rachel joined Mr Bruff on the journey back to London. By eleven o'clock that morning the house in Yorkshire was again quiet and empty.

❖

When they arrived in London, Mr Bruff was met at the station by a small boy. He was a poor boy. His clothes were old and worn, and he had a strange-looking face with large, round eyes.

He saw Rachel kneeling beside him.

'This is Gooseberry,' said Mr Bruff. 'He may have strange-looking eyes, but this boy notices everything, and he's quick. He has brought us some interesting news – Mr Luker is on his way to the bank.'

Bruff and Franklin quickly said goodbye to Rachel, and got into a **cab** with Gooseberry. They hurried across town to the bank in Lombard Street. Franklin looked at the people in the bank, but he couldn't see the Indians anywhere. The only person with dark skin was a tall man with a thick, dark beard, and a sailor's hat and coat.

'Perhaps, he's working as a spy for the Indians,' thought Franklin.

cab taxi

Mr Luker came out of an office, and slowly made his way to the door of the bank. Franklin and Bruff watched him carefully. As Mr Luker walked past a man in a grey suit, they both saw Mr Luker's hand move. Had Mr Luker given him something?

Gooseberry had already disappeared, so they decided to follow the man in the grey suit. When the man had finished his business at the bank, Bruff and Franklin followed him onto a bus. They got off with the man in Oxford Street, and followed him to a shop that sold medicine. Mr Bruff knew the shop owner and learnt from him that they had followed the wrong man.

'The man in the grey suit is a shop assistant,' said Bruff. 'I'm sure he knows nothing about the Moonstone. Let's hope that Gooseberry is doing a better job than us!'

While Franklin and Bruff had followed an innocent man, Gooseberry had followed the tall sailor with a dark face. Gooseberry noticed Mr Luker pass something to him, and as the sailor quickly left the bank, Gooseberry followed him. The sailor got into a cab, Gooseberry jumped on the back, and they went to Tower **Wharf**.

At the wharf, a **steamboat** was preparing to leave for Rotterdam the next morning. But the sailor didn't get on the ship. Instead he went into a cheap restaurant nearby. Gooseberry waited outside and saw a mechanic standing on the other side of the road. As Gooseberry watched, a cab came by and stopped in front of the mechanic. Someone put his head out of the cab to talk to the mechanic – someone with a dark face like an Indian – and a few minutes later the cab drove away.

After he had eaten, the tall sailor went to a pub called *The Wheel of Fortune*. Gooseberry followed him into the pub, and so did the mechanic. The tall man asked the **landlord** for a room for the night, and the landlord gave him room number ten. It was a small room at the top of the house. A servant took the sailor up to the room. Gooseberry decided to wait a little before he left the pub so he sat down.

wharf a place on a river that boats arrive at and leave from

steamboat a boat that is powered by steam from burning coal

landlord the owner of a pub

Just then, there was a lot of noise upstairs. The landlord went to see what the noise was about, and a few minutes later came back with the mechanic. The mechanic was drunk and was trying to get into room number ten. The mechanic was thrown out of the pub, but when Gooseberry followed him down the street, he noticed that the man was not really drunk at all. But by now it was late, and Gooseberry went home.

At ten o'clock the next morning, Gooseberry went straight to Franklin Blake's house to report what he had seen. He was taken into the sitting room, but stopped when he saw that Franklin had a visitor – an older, sad-looking man.

'Come in, Gooseberry,' said Franklin. 'This is Sergeant Cuff. He has come to help us solve the mystery! Please report everything to us.'

Gooseberry had heard of the famous Sergeant Cuff, and he told his story with great excitement. Sergeant Cuff was sure that Gooseberry had followed the right man, and ten minutes later the three of them were in a cab on their way to *The Wheel of Fortune*.

When they arrived at the pub, the landlord was hurrying down the stairs.

'What do you want?' he said angrily, when he saw them.

'I am Sergeant Cuff, and we've come to ask about a man who stayed here last night,' explained Cuff. 'A tall, dark man dressed in sailor's clothes.'

The landlord also recognized the name of this famous detective, and spoke more politely.

'I'm very pleased that you are here, sir. The man you are looking for has been troubling us. We've been calling him since seven o'clock this morning but he doesn't answer.

'Do you think he's left without paying?' asked Cuff.

'Well, it is possible, I suppose,' explained the landlord. 'Room number ten is at the top of the building and there's a small door in the ceiling into the roof. If he climbed through the door onto the roof, he could then get into the house next door, which is empty.

That way, he could easily leave without paying.'

After that, the landlord went to fetch a **saw**. Then, with Cuff and Franklin, he went back up to room number ten and started to cut through the door. Then, the three men pushed, and pushed the door until at last they broke into the room.

The tall sailor had not left the room. He was still in bed – with a **pillow** over his face. The landlord removed the pillow and there under it a dark face, with its eyes wide open, was staring up at them.

'He's dead!' shouted the landlord. 'Fetch a doctor.'

Gooseberry had followed the men into the room. He didn't seem worried about the dead man. He was pointing excitedly at a small wooden box on a small table next to the bed. The box was empty. With the box there was a banker's receipt. It said that the box belonged to Mr Luker.

'Robbery!' shouted Gooseberry. 'And murder!'

Sergeant Cuff looked at the man again and noticed a thin white line between the top of his dark face and his hair. Cuff took hold of the man's hair and pulled. The hair came off in his hands. It was a **wig**. Then Cuff took the man's beard off, and then he took some water and a towel and started washing the man's face. It became clear that the dark skin was also part of the strange **disguise**.

Franklin couldn't believe his eyes. The face of the man in front of him was that of Godfrey Ablewhite. It didn't seem possible, but it was true.

Later that morning, a doctor came to examine the dead body and declared that Godfrey Ablewhite's death was indeed a murder. Someone – or a group of people – had held the pillow over Mr Ablewhite's nose and mouth in order to kill him. When they asked Mr Luker about the box on the table beside the bed, he said that it had contained the Moonstone diamond. Everyone agreed that someone – or a group of people – had murdered Godfrey Ablewhite in order to steal the Moonstone from him.

saw a metal knife with teeth that is used to cut

pillow the soft thing on your bed that you put your head on when you sleep

wig false hair

disguise something that you wear so that people cannot recognize you

And everyone agreed that the murderer or murderers were most probably the Indians.

Sergeant Cuff made further investigations and discovered that the Indians had entered room number ten through the small door in the ceiling. They had come through the roof of the empty house next door, and had moved silently onto the roof of the pub, and down into the room where Godfrey Ablewhite was sleeping. They knew that he was there because the mechanic, who was their spy, had told them. A small piece of gold cloth was found in room number ten. It was the kind of cloth that was not made or sold anywhere in England. The only place to find such cloth was India.

The same morning that Godfrey Ablewhite was found dead, the three Indians were seen in Tower Wharf. They were getting onto the steamboat which was sailing to Rotterdam. It was the beginning of their long journey back to India. They were taking the Moonstone back to the place where it belonged.

They were taking the Moonstone back to the place where it belonged.

READING CHECK

What do they say? Match the sentences with the speakers.

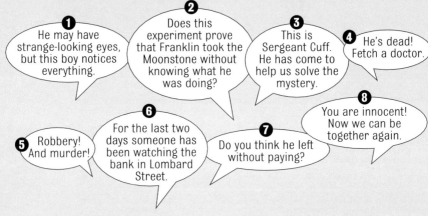

❶ He may have strange-looking eyes, but this boy notices everything.

❷ Does this experiment prove that Franklin took the Moonstone without knowing what he was doing?

❸ This is Sergeant Cuff. He has come to help us solve the mystery.

❹ He's dead! Fetch a doctor.

❺ Robbery! And murder!

❻ For the last two days someone has been watching the bank in Lombard Street.

❼ Do you think he left without paying?

❽ You are innocent! Now we can be together again.

a ⟦2⟧ . . . asks Ezra Jennings.

b ☐ . . . says Rachel.

c ☐ . . . explains Mr Bruff.

d ☐ . . . Mr Bruff says about Gooseberry.

e ☐ . . . says Franklin to Gooseberry.

f ☐ . . . Sergeant Cuff asks the landlord

g ☐ . . . shouts the landlord.

h ☐ . . . shouts Gooseberry.

WORD WORK

Write words from Chapter 9 to match the pictures.

a l a n d l o r d

b p _ _ _ _ _

c s _ _ _ _ _ _ _ _

d s _ _

e c _ _

f w _ _

g w _ _ _ _

h d _ _ _ _ _ _ _

GUESS WHAT

In the last chapter we find out what happened to the Moonstone. What do you think? Tick the boxes.

a Godfrey got the Moonstone because . . .

 1 ☐ he found it on the floor.

 2 ☐ Franklin gave it to him when he was sleep-walking.

 3 ☐ he took it from Franklin's room.

b Godfrey decided to keep the Moonstone because . . .

 1 ☐ he had a lot of debts to pay.

 2 ☐ he was angry when Rachel refused to marry him.

 3 ☐ he wanted to give it to his lover.

c Godfrey took the Moonstone to Mr Luker in order to . . .

 1 ☐ hide it from the Indians.

 2 ☐ sell it.

 3 ☐ borrow money.

d Godfrey was planning to . . .

 1 ☐ take the Moonstone back to India.

 2 ☐ take the Moonstone to Amsterdam.

 3 ☐ have the Moonstone made into a necklace.

Chapter 10

The mystery is solved

Sergeant Cuff and Mr Bruff continued their investigations after Godfrey Ablewhite's death. With some important information from Mr Luker, they were able to find out how and why Godfrey had stolen the diamond.

Godfrey Ablewhite had had a **respectable** job, and was well-known for his charity work and for helping poor people. But his death uncovered another – secret – side of Godfrey's life. He had also owned a large **villa** on the edge of London. The villa was full of fine pictures, statues, and beautiful furniture. A beautiful young woman, Godfrey's lover, lived in the house. She had many expensive clothes and jewels. Over the years Godfrey had paid for everything: the villa, the pictures and the jewels. But where had the money come from?

Some years before, in his work as a lawyer, Godfrey had received a large sum of money to keep safely for a young **client**. The client had inherited a fortune of £20,000, but was unable to receive the money until he reached the age of twenty-one. Twice a year Godfrey had to pay his client an income of £300, and in February 1850, Godfrey had to return the £20,000 to his client. Although the money did not belong to Godfrey, he had **forged** cheques in order to spend it. By the end of 1847, he had spent every penny of his client's fortune to pay for the villa and everything it contained. He was also no longer able to pay the twice-yearly income of £300 to his client.

On the day of Rachel's birthday party, Godfrey had seen her birthday present from Colonel Herncastle. Because he realized how valuable the diamond was, Godfrey had asked Rachel to marry him that afternoon. But Rachel was in love with Franklin, so she had refused him. That night, Godfrey was unable to sleep because his money troubles were keeping him awake. He heard Franklin walking outside his room. He got up and saw Franklin

respectable that people think is good

villa a house in the country with a large garden, especially in Southern Europe

client customer

forge to sign something pretending to be another person

walking towards Rachel's room with a candle. He followed
Franklin, and watched him through the open door of Rachel's
sitting room. He saw Franklin take the Moonstone and he could
see that Rachel was watching him, too, from her bedroom door.
When Franklin left Rachel's sitting room, he walked back to his
own room and met Godfrey there.

'Take this to Frizinghall,' Franklin said to Godfrey. 'It's not safe

*He saw Franklin
take the
Moonstone.*

here. I'm too tired to move. Take it at once!'

In the morning Godfrey realized that Franklin didn't remember anything about the night before. From Rachel's behaviour, Godfrey saw that Rachel knew Franklin had taken her diamond. Godfrey left for London with the Moonstone as soon as possible and went straight to Mr Luker. Mr Luker examined the jewel carefully.

'How did you come by this?' he asked Godfrey. 'And I only want to hear the truth! I cannot help you if you do not tell me the truth.'

Godfrey needed to borrow money and he told Mr Luker that Franklin had given him the jewel. Mr Luker then agreed to lend him £2,000 and to keep the diamond for a year. A few weeks before the day that Godfrey had to pay back his debt to Mr Luker, he went abroad to Amsterdam. There he arranged to have the diamond cut up into smaller stones. If he sold the stones, he could make more than £20,000 – enough to pay his client on his twenty-first birthday.

Godfrey's plan was going very well. But he had forgotten one thing – the Indian priests. The priests had already lost two chances to recover their diamond. They had waited a long time for this third chance, and they did not fail again. They finally got the diamond and took it home.

❖

And so the Indian guard was right when he had warned John Herncastle about the revenge of the Moonstone; the diamond had nearly destroyed his family. But Franklin and Rachel were strong and determined. They had solved the mystery, and soon after Franklin's innocence was proved, he and Rachel were engaged. The wedding ceremony took place at the house in Yorkshire on 9th October 1849, and old Gabriel Betteredge was the happiest servant in England.

❖

And where was the Moonstone now? Six months later, Mr Bruff received a letter from Mr Murthwaite.

February 1850

Dear Mr Bruff,

Since we last spoke after dinner in the autumn of 1848, I have been travelling in Asia. In our conversation we spoke about the Moonstone. I am writing to you now with news of that jewel.

I was travelling towards the city of Somnauth in southern India. On the way I met many people who were travelling to the same place. They were **Hindu pilgrims** on their way to a special ceremony at Somnauth.

I disguised myself as a Hindu and joined the pilgrims in order to witness the ceremony. On the night of the full moon, I went with hundreds of pilgrims to a hill outside the city. On top of the hill there was a big flat rock, and on the rock was a small shrine covered with some cloth.

The **ceremony** began and three Hindu priests came onto the rock. I recognised them immediately. They were the same Indians that we saw in the garden of the Verinders' house in Yorkshire on the evening of Miss Rachel's birthday party. The men knelt down in front of the **shrine** and took off the cloth.

There in front of us was the statue of the Moon God, and in the **forehead** of the statue was the yellow diamond - the same one that Miss Rachel had worn on her dress!

After three long centuries the Moonstone adventure is over. The jewel is back in the place where it belongs, and it will never be seen in England again.

pilgrim a person who travels to a religious place

Hindu a religion that is common in India and parts of Asia

ceremony something you do to recognise a special event

shrine a small, special place for a statue of a god

forehead the part of your face above your eyes

ACTIVITIES

READING CHECK

Circle the words to complete the sentences.

a Godfrey Ablewhite secretly owned a beautiful house where his (lover) / wife / mother lived.

b Godfrey used his father's / Rachel's / his client's fortune to buy a beautiful house for himself.

c Godfrey wanted to marry Rachel because she could help him sign more cheques. / solve his money problems / give more money to charit

d Godfrey knew that Rachel saw him take the diamond from Franklin. / Franklin give the diamond to him. / Franklin take the diamond.

e Mr Luker agreed to pay / lend / give Godfrey £2,000 for the Moonstone.

f The Indian priests took the Moonstone to Amsterdam. / to Mr Murthwaite. / back to India.

WORD WORK

Find words in the puzzle to complete the sentences.

cli	for	shr	able	du
Hin	pil	ect	lla	grims
resp	cere	ent	ge	mony
he	vi	fore	ad	ine

a Lady Verinder was Mr Bruff's ....client....; she paid him to be her lawyer.

b No one suspected Godfrey Ablewhite because he had a .... job.

c Ezra Jennings looked old because he had a wrinkled .... and white hair.

d They had a large house in London, and a .... near the sea.

e Shah Jehan built the Taj Mahal as a .... to the memory of his dead wife.

f Vishnu is one of the many gods of the .... religion.

g Every year, thousands of Muslim .... visit Mecca in Saudi Arabia.

h There is a special .... every year to remember the people who were killed at war.

i It is against the law to .... someone else's papers.

WHAT NEXT?

The Moonstone was one of the first detective stories, and Wilkie Collins was one of the first detective story writers. Here are two more famous crime writers.

Agatha Christie
(1890–1976)
wrote stories
about Miss Marple
and Hercule Poirot.

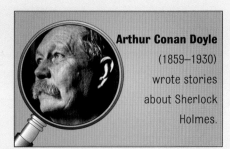

Arthur Conan Doyle
(1859–1930)
wrote stories
about Sherlock
Holmes.

1 Which of these stories were written by Agatha Christie and which were written by Arthur Conan Doyle?

2 Which of these stories would you like to read? Why?

Project A   *Indian Festivals*

1   Match the words and the pictures.

a ☐ drums

b ☐ paint powder

c ☐ fireworks

d ☐ a bonfire

e ☐ an elephant

f ☐ parasols

g ☐ ash

2   Read the information about the Pooram Festival and answer the questions on page 73.

The Pooram Festival takes place at the end of April or the beginning of May.

'Pooram' means a meeting, and people believe that this was the day when the gods met to celebrate the spring.

Today the celebrations take place outside a temple in Thrissur. There are

Pooram Festival

two lines of thirteen elephants. The elephants are brightly decorated and the elephant riders make a colourful display with parasols. In front of the elephants, drummers and other musicians play very loud music.

Hundreds of people gather to watch and they cheer the elephant riders when they change the parasol display.

The festival ends late at night with a fantastic fireworks display.

Pooram Festival, at Thrissur, southern India

a Where does the festival take place?

b When does the festival take place?

c What do people watch?

3 Use the notes about the Holi festival to complete the website information.

when?	three days in March
where?	all over India, especially northern India
what celebrate?	arrival of spring
how long last?	three days
what people do?	throw paint powder, smear paint on each other, light bonfires, take ash from the bonfire

Holi Festival, India

Holi festival lasts for **(a)** .... days at the end of March. The festival takes place all over India, but it is especially popular in **(b)** .... India. At the festival, people use colour to celebrate the **(c)** .... People enjoy throwing **(d)** .... around and they also **(e)** .... each other with paint. In the evenings they light **(f)** .... People walk around the bonfire seven times and ask for good luck. When the bonfire is finished, they take some of the **(g)** .... and put it on the foreheads of their children. They believe that the ash will protect the children from illness.

4 Make notes about a festival that takes place in your town or country in a table like the one above. Write the text.

Project B   *Famous Indian Diamonds*

1 Read the story of the Hope diamond. Complete the text with the missing information.

Hindu statue   Henry Hope   France $180,000

King George   Hope diamond   1947   car accident

twenty-five   Smithsonian Institution

The Hope Diamond

In 1911, a rich young American woman, Evalyn Walsh McLean, was visiting Paris with her husband. The jeweller Pierre Cartier met the couple at their hotel. He showed them a beautiful large blue diamond and told interesting stories about it.

'The jewel was taken from a **(a)** .... and everyone who has worn it has had bad luck,' he explained. People believe that this diamond was owned by King Louis XIV of France, and that it disappeared from **(b)** .... during the French Revolution in 1792. Forty years later the diamond appeared in a painting around the neck of the English King George IV. No one knew how **(c)** .... had got the jewel, but everyone believed that it was the 'French Blue' diamond. In 1839, a rich London banker called **(d)** .... became the owner of the diamond, and from that time it was called the Hope diamond. The Hope family later sold it to pay their debts.

Evalyn thought that the diamond was wonderfully mysterious, and she bought it for **(e)** .... She lived an expensive life in Washington, and at all her parties she wore the **(f)** .... and told its story. Soon the beautiful blue jewel was famous.

But bad things began to happen to Evalyn. Her nine-year-old son was killed in a **(g)** ....; her husband left her for another woman and died from drinking too much alcohol; her daughter killed herself at the age of **(h)** .... When Evalyn died in **(i)** .... the diamond was sold to pay her debts.

You can see the diamond today in the museum of the **(j)** ....

**2 Put the sentences in the correct order to tell the story of the Orloff diamond.
Number them 1–9.**

The Orloff Diamond

This large white diamond is as big as half a chicken's egg. Like the Moonstone, it came from the forehead of a statue in a Hindu temple in Mysore, southern India . . .

a ☐ Orloff wanted to give it as a present to the woman he loved Catherine the Great of Russia.

b ☐ Today you can see the Orloff diamond in the Kremlin in Moscow.

c ☐ The Frenchman lived in Mysore disguised as a Hindu, and went to ceremonies at the temple there for some years.

d ☐ His ship went though a terrible storm on the way, but he lived though it and sold the diamond to a jeweller in Madras.

e ☐ In 1755, a rich Russian Count, Grigory Orloff, bought the diamond from a Dutch jeweller for $450,000.

f ☐ The Madras jeweller soon sold the wonderful stone, and after that the diamond was bought and sold many times; five years later it reached Amsterdam.

g ☐ The story begins with a young Frenchman who ran away from the French army in India.

h ☐ Although Catherine loved the diamond, she did not fall in love with Count Orloff. But she did give Orloff's name to the famous diamond.

i ☐ In 1750, he stole the diamond from the statue in the temple and took a ship to Madras.

3 Find information about another famous Indian diamond. Write the story.

The Koh-i-Noor Diamond

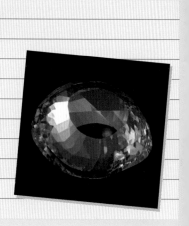

The Regent Diamond

GRAMMAR CHECK

Reported speech with tell

We use the verb tell to report commands and statements. We must use an indirect object after tell in reported speech.

Reported command = tell someone to do something

Direct command: *'Get a room ready for Franklin,' Lady Verinder said to Betteredge.*

Reported command: *Lady Verinder told Betteredge to get a room ready for Franklin.*

Reported statement = tell someone (that) + statement

Direct statement: *'I'm not arriving until dinner time,' Franklin said to them.*

Reported statement: *Franklin had told them that he wasn't arriving until dinner time.*

In reported speech, verbs go one step into the past. Personal pronouns and possessive adjectives change to match the subject of the reported speech sentence.

1 Rewrite direct speech as reported speech with *tell*.

a 'The Indians want to do something wicked,' Penelope said to her father.

Penelope told her father that the Indians wanted to do something wicked.

b 'Come and sit down,' Betteredge said to Rosanna.

....

c 'My uncle has left the diamond as a birthday present to Rachel,' Franklin said to Betteredge.

....

d 'Take the diamond to Rachel in Yorkshire,' Franklin's father said to him.

....

e 'Your uncle never tried to sell the jewel,' Betteredge said to Franklin.

....

f 'I'll remember my niece's birthday!' Herncastle said to them two years before.

....

g 'Take the Moonstone to Amsterdam,' the letter told Bruff.

....

h 'He left it to show that he forgives Lady Verinder,' Franklin said to Betteredge.

....

Present Perfect Simple and Present Perfect Continuous

We can use the Present Perfect Simple to describe finished actions that took place at some time in the past, but which still have an effect on the present.

Rosanna has fallen in love with Franklin.

We use the Present Perfect Continuous to describe activities that started in the past and are still continuing in the present.

Rosanna has been behaving very strangely.

Some verbs – for example *see*, *hear*, and *know* – cannot usually be used in the Continuous form. They are known as 'stative' verbs.

2 Complete the sentences with the verbs in brackets in the Present Perfect or the Present Perfect Continuous.

a Rosanna ...*has been working*... (work) for Lady Verinder as a housemaid since she left prison.

b Franklin .... (come) back from abroad. He .... (stay) at Lady Verinder's house for a month now.

c Rachel is the most charming girl Franklin .... (ever / meet).

d While Franklin and Rachel .... (paint) the door to her sitting room, the servants .... (talk) about them.

e Franklin .... (stop) smoking to please Rachel.

f They .... (not see) the Indians again.

g Rachel .... (never / tell) her secrets to anyone, not even her mother.

h Why .... (John Herncastle / leave) the Moonstone as a gift for Rachel?

i Rachel .... (refuse) to marry Godfrey because she is in love with another man.

j Lady Verinder .... (feel) worried about her brother's gift for Rachel. .... (he / forgive) her, or is he looking for revenge?

GRAMMAR CHECK

Verb + gerund or infinitive with to

After the verbs *continue*, *agree*, *decide*, *plan*, *refuse*, and *try* we use infinitive with *to*.

Although Franklin was sleeping badly, he refused to take any medicine.

After the verbs *finish*, *remember*, *start*, and *stop* we use verb + –ing.

At the dinner party, Dr Candy and Franklin started arguing about medicine.

3 Complete the sentences using *to* + infinitive or the gerund form of the verb in brackets.

a After the servants had left, Detective Seagrave continued ..to examine. (examine) Rachel's room.

b Rachel and Franklin had finished .... (paint) the door at three o'clock in the afternoon on the day of her birthday party.

c The next day, Sergeant Cuff planned .... (go) to Frizinghall.

d When she left, Rachel refused .... (say) goodbye to Franklin.

e Franklin went back to London, but he couldn't stop .... (think) about Rachel. He decided .... (go) abroad and try .... (forget) everything.

f People started ....(talk) about the news of the strange attack on Godfrey Ablewhite.

g On the day of her birthday, Rachel and Godfrey agreed .... (be) friends.

h Franklin didn't remember .... (take) the diamond, but the evidence pointed to him.

i When Franklin and Betteredge finished .... (read) Rosanna's letter, they were deep in thought.

j Franklin decided .... (take) the letter and nightgown to Mr Bruff.

k When Rachel saw Franklin, she stopped .... (play) the piano.

l Franklin agreed .... (do) the experiment, but first he had to stop .... (smoke).

GRAMMAR CHECK

If clauses with will, must, and can

We can use *if* clauses to describe a possible future action which can happen as a result of another action. We always use the Present Simple in this type of if clause and we use *will* (or a modal verb, like *must* or *can*) in the main clause.

When the if clause comes at the start of the sentence, we put a comma after it.

If you borrow money, you must pay back the debt in a year.

When the if clause comes at the end of the sentence, we don't put a comma before it.

You must pay back the debt in a year if you borrow money.

4 **Complete these sentences with the verbs in brackets in the correct form. Then write in the box the name of the character who says each sentence.**

Betteredge	~~Franklin~~	Murthwaite
Ezra Jennings	Mr Bruff	Sergeant Cuff

a 'I .can't sleep. well if I don't smoke,' said Franklin. (can't sleep / not smoke)

b 'Rachel, if priests in India .... you with that diamond, they .... you!' said .... (see / kill)

c 'If Rosanna .... the diamond, she .... it to a jeweller in London,' said .... (have / take)

d 'If anyone .... on this part of the beach, the sand .... them down,' said .... (step / pull)

e 'If Rachel .... that Godfrey is innocent, it .... true!' said .... (say / must be)

f 'If Godfrey .... you, he .... a large sum of money. He knows that, Rachel,' said .... (marry / not get)

g 'If we .... who borrowed Mr Luker's money, we .... the person who took the diamond,' said .... (discover / find)

h 'If Franklin .... the experiment, he .... us where the jewel is,' said .... (do / show)

GRAMMAR CHECK

Will or Going to Future

We make the *will* Future tense using will + infinitive without *to*. We make the *going to* Future with the verb be + going to + infinitive.

We can use *will* and *going to* to describe future actions. We use *will* to talk about predictions and things that we aren't sure about. We often use adverbs like *maybe*, *perhaps*, and *probably* with the *will* Future. We use the *going to* Future to talk about plans and intentions and for predictions where there is evidence now.

I'm going to solve the mystery. Then perhaps she will speak to me again.

5 **Complete the pairs of sentences about Chapter 8 with two of the verbs in brackets. Complete one sentence with *will* and one sentence with *going to*.**

a Ezra is going to help Franklin because he hopes that Franklin will have a happier life than his own. (help / have / be)

b Ezra .... Franklin opium again. He thinks that Franklin .... what he did on the night the diamond was taken. (prove / give / repeat)

c Franklin .... the experiment. He hopes that it .... his innocence. (make / do / prove)

d Rachel and Mr Bruff .... the experiment secretly. Rachel hopes that she and Franklin .... together again. (watch / do / be)

e Mr Bruff .... a witness. Franklin .... that he is there. (be / know / not know)

f Betteredge .... Lady Verinder's house for the experiment. The experiment .... if things are different. (prepare / not prepare / not work)

g Mr Bruff .... someone to watch the bank in London. Perhaps they .... who borrowed money from Mr Luker. (help / send / find out)

h Ezra .... Dr Candy about the experiment. Dr Candy probably .... anything. (tell / not tell / not remember)

Causative make

We form causative make with make + object + infinitive without *to*, or with make + object + adjective.

We use causative make to talk about something we do although we don't want to do it.

You made me kiss you!   Opium makes you sleepy.

6 **Match sentence halves a–i with 1–9. Write complete sentences using *make*.**

a Franklin's opinion about medicine ⟨9⟩

    Franklin's opinion about medicine made Dr Candy angry.

b The fact that Rachel was wearing the diamond at the party ☐

    ....

c When Detective Seagrave put policemen to guard the rooms, it ☐

    ....

d Franklin's words to Sergeant Cuff ☐

    ....

e The attack on Godfrey Ablewhite ☐

    ....

f Godfrey was a good speaker and he ☐

    ....

g Godfrey's parents wanted to ☐

    ....

h Rosanna ☐

    ....

i Mr Luker ☐

    ....

1 Rachel agree to marry him.	**6** people suspect that he had stolen the diamond.
2 Godfrey tell him the truth.	
3 Rosanna deeply unhappy.	**7** Lady Verinder very worried.
4 the servants angry.	**8** Rachel feel as comfortable as possible.
5 Limping Lucy deliver the letter to Franklin in person.	**9** ~~Dr Candy angry.~~

GRAMMAR

GRAMMAR CHECK

Past Simple and Past Perfect

We use the Past Simple to talk about past actions that follow each other in a story.

Gooseberry followed the men into the room and pointed at the empty box on the table.

We use the Past Perfect for actions that happened *before* an action in the past.

Sergeant Cuff and Mr Bruff found out how and why Godfrey had stolen the diamond.

             (second action)   (first action)

7 **Complete the text with the verbs in the box in the Past Simple or Past Perfect. Use the Past Perfect where possible.**

agree	ask	believe	forge	forget	get up	give	go	realize	receive
refuse	not remember	see	see	spend	take	tell	~~work~~		

When Godfrey a) <u>worked</u> as a lawyer, he b) .... a large sum of money to keep safe. Instead of looking after the money, he c) .... cheques and he d) .... every penny. When Godfrey e) .... Rachel's diamond, he f) .... how valuable it was. Godfrey g) .... Rachel to marry him but she h) .... because she was in love with Franklin.

That night Godfrey couldn't sleep. He i) .... and he j) .... Franklin taking the Moonstone. On the way back to his room Franklin k) .... Godfrey the diamond, but in the morning he l) .... anything about it. Godfrey knew from Rachel's behaviour that she m) .... Franklin n) .... her diamond.

The next morning Godfrey o) .... straight to Mr Luker's with the diamond. After Godfrey p) .... him the truth, he q) .... to keep the diamond for a year. Godfrey's plan was going well, but he r) .... one thing – the Indian priests.

83

Dominoes is an enjoyable series of illustrated classic and modern stories in four carefully graded language stages – from Starter to Three – which take learners from beginner to intermediate level.

Each *Domino* reader includes:

- **a good story** to read and enjoy
- **integrated activities** to develop reading skills and increase active vocabulary
- **personalized projects** to make the language and story themes more meaningful
- **seven pages of grammar activities** for consolidation.

Each *Domino* pack contains a reader, plus a MultiROM with:

- **a complete audio recording of the story**, fully dramatized to bring it to life
- **interactive activities** to offer further practice in reading and language skills and to consolidate learning.

If you liked this Level Three *Domino*, why not read these?

Mansfield Park
Jane Austen

'Why shouldn't we offer to take care of her? She could live with us at Mansfield.'

In this way Mrs Norris persuades her sister, Lady Bertram, and Lady Bertram's husband, Sir Thomas, to ask their poor niece Fanny Price to live with them at Mansfield Park.

At first Fanny is unhappy there. Then, after she makes friends with her young cousins, things improve. But what happens when the cousins are older, and starting to think of love?

Book ISBN: 978 0 19 424828 0
MultiROM Pack ISBN: 978 0 19 424786 3

The Count of Monte Cristo
Alexandre Dumas

Marseille, France, 1815. It is Edmond Dantès' wedding day. But his enemies have other plans, and Edmond is arrested and sent to the terrible island prison of Château d'If. For fourteen long years he waits for the right moment to escape.

And now Edmond is a rich man, with many disguises, and a new name. The Count of Monte Cristo begins his revenge…

Book ISBN: 978 0 19 424819 8
MultiROM Pack ISBN: 978 0 19 424777 1

You can find details and a full list of books in the *Dominoes* catalogue and Oxford English Language Teaching Catalogue, and on the website: www.oup.com/elt

Teachers: see www.oup.com/elt for a full range of online support, or consult your local office.

	CEF	Cambridge Exams	IELTS	TOEFL iBT	TOEIC
Starter	A1	YLE Movers	–	–	–
Level 1	A1–A2	YLE Flyers/KET	3.0	–	–
Level 2	A2–B1	KET-PET	3.0-4.0	–	–
Level 3	B1	PET	4.0	57-86	550